Through the Eyes of the Enemy

THROUGH THE EYES OF THE ENEMY:

Russia's highest ranking military defector reveals why Russia is more dangerous than ever

Stanislav Lunev with Ira Winkler

Regnery Publishing, Inc.
Washington, D.C.

COPYRIGHT © 1998 STANISLAV LUNEV AND IRA WINKLER

All rights reserved. No part of this publication may be reproduced or transmitted in any form or by any means electronic or mechanical, including photocopy, recording, or any information storage and retrieval system now known or to be invented, without permission in writing from the publisher, except by a reviewer who wishes to quote brief passages in connection with a review written for inclusion in a magazine, newspaper, or broadcast.

Library of Congress Cataloging-in-Publication Data
Lunev, Stanislav, 1946–
    Through the eyes of the enemy : Russia's highest ranking military defector reveals why Russia is more dangerous than ever / by Stanislav Lunev, with Ira Winkler.

                    p.   cm.
    Includes index.
    ISBN 0-89526-390-4 (alk. paper)
    1. Lunev, Stanislav, 1946–   . 2. Defectors--Soviet Union--Biography. 3. Spies--Soviet Union--Biography. 4. Soviet Union Glavnoe razvedyvatel' noe upravlenie--Officals and employees--Biography. 5. Espionage, Soviet. 6. Soviet Union--History--1953-1985. 7. Soviet Union--History--1985–1991.
    I. Winkler, Ira. II. Title.
    UB271.R92L865   1998
    327.1247'092--dc21
    [B]   98-7203
                                                               CIP

Published in the United States by
Regnery Publishing, Inc.
One Massachusetts Avenue, NW
Washington, DC 20001

Distributed to the trade by
National Book Network
4720-A Boston Way
Lanham, MD 20706

Printed on acid-free paper.
Manufactured in the United States of America

10 9 8 7 6 5 4 3 2 1

Books are available in quantity for promotional or premium use. Write to Director of Special Sales, Regnery Publishing, Inc., One Massachusetts Avenue, NW, Washington, DC 20001, for information on discounts and terms or call (202) 216-0600.

To my loving wife Natalie, who put up with more than anybody could ever have imagined.
—Stanislav

To Molly, thanks and love.
—Ira

CONTENTS

CHAPTER 1   Target: America   *11*

CHAPTER 2   My Military Childhood   *35*

CHAPTER 3   America, the Enemy   *41*

CHAPTER 4   Tactics and Strategy   *49*

CHAPTER 5   Hungary: Learning to Penetrate Enemy Lines   *57*

CHAPTER 6   Military Justice   *65*

CHAPTER 7   Training and Terrorism   *71*

CHAPTER 8   Singapore   *85*

CHAPTER 9   Learning the Craft   *95*

CHAPTER 10   China   *101*

CHAPTER 11   Assignment: America   *121*

CHAPTER 12   My "Arrival"   *125*

CHAPTER 13   World War III   *137*

CHAPTER 14   My Spies   *143*

CHAPTER 15   A Coup in Moscow, A New Life in America   *155*

DEBRIEFING ONE   Israel   *163*

DEBRIEFING TWO   POWs in Vietnam   *167*

INDEX   *173*

Acknowledgments

There are many well-deserving people we would like to acknowledge, but for their own benefit we won't.

Chapter 1

TARGET: AMERICA

AS A FORMER COLONEL in the GRU—the military counterpart of the KGB (now called the SVR)—I am the GRU's highest ranking Soviet defector to the United States. For six years I have cooperated with the CIA, the FBI, and other American intelligence organizations. For the most part, I have done so quietly, under the shield of the witness protection program. But I have had a brush with death. Cancer struck me, as it has struck—surprisingly or not so surprisingly, given our world of sophisticated assassination and poisoning—almost all my colleagues who worked at the Russian embassy in China. But unlike so many of them, I have survived. I have no fear of death now whether it comes from cancer or from a paid Russian assassin. But I do feel I have an obligation to use my experience to warn America of the dirty tricks that can be played against her. And if I have one message for my adopted country, it is this: the Cold War is not over; the new cold war is between the Russian mafia and the United States; and in this new cold war, the Russian mafia has every tool, every weapon, every intelligence asset at its disposal that the old Soviet Union had. America is facing a nation led by gangsters—gangsters who have nuclear weapons. And some of those weapons are actually on American soil, as I will explain.

When the Soviet Union collapsed and its industries were privatized, there was only one group within Russia with the money to buy the new industries, and that was the Russian mafia. But the mafia did more than buy the industries—it bought the government.

That's why I defected, because as a career Russian military intelligence officer in the GRU, I believed in serving my country—not organized crime or the tools of organized crime, like Boris Yeltsin, who has ordered the GRU and the rest of the intelligence apparatus to make commercial and industrial espionage its primary mission.

Today, American business is the chief target of the GRU, the SVR, and the entire network of Russian spies. Their paymaster is the Russian mafia. Their goal is to make Russian mobsters rich. Compared to the military operations we used to run, the work is easy.

For every one person who will surrender military secrets, a good agent can acquire three to five people to give him industrial secrets. In the first place, many companies don't realize the value of their secrets, which can be found sitting in unlocked file cabinets, on insecure computers, or on someone's desk. Most secrets in Western companies are easy to steal. Many Americans dislike their jobs. It takes very little to convince a disgruntled employee to transfer information that might just as well have gone into a wastepaper basket.

Relatively few people are arrested for giving commercial secrets to foreign intelligence officers. Most who are caught are merely fired. Certainly in the West, none are killed. So the risks are few.

Moreover, industrial espionage does not require recruiting agents. Russian signal intelligence is capable of intercepting telephone calls, satellite communications, and microwave and cellular transmissions from all over the United States. Russian computer specialists are trained to hack into computers all over the world. In fact, every company that is on the Internet can be penetrated by Russian hackers. The Internet is just one way to get into companies. Computer security is as bad, if not worse, as the physical security inside most companies.

The Cold War is not over; the new Cold War is between the Russian mafia and the United States.

If this isn't bad enough, Russia and China have signed agreements to share economic and military intelligence. From a military perspective, Russia provided China with details of where U.S. warships were during recent Chinese war games near Taiwan. From a commercial perspective, the Chinese want Russian information on Western satellite systems, which they can use to modernize their own satellites and sell them to the third world.

What is critical for America to understand is how the Russian mafia provides assignments for Russian and Chinese intelligence. The Russian Ministry of Defense and the Ministry of Defense Industry set the objectives for the GRU and the SVR. Executives from Russian defense companies attend meetings of the Ministry of Defense Industry. When they bring up a possible target, the GRU and SVR ask how much they are willing to pay for the information. If the amount is large enough, they accept the job. Then the SVR and GRU compete to see who will get the information first. Whoever gets the best lead is then given the mission. When the information is successfully gathered, the payoff from the mafia-run business is delivered. Of course, the senior people in the intelligence agencies take their cuts.

While there is no big reward for the people who actually obtain the information, this capitalistic approach to intelligence ensures that the intelligence operatives get paid at a time when few other people in the Russian military are.

Indeed, the whole death-grip on the Russian government comes from the Russian mafia's control of the economy. That control started in the depths of the communist regime. Russian organized crime offered protection for Russia's thriving black market, which they eventually controlled. It grew so profitable that the mafia, in due course, filled the power void created by Gorbachev's *perestroika*.

The Soviet Union did not collapse because of "reform minded leaders" or because of the Reagan administration's brilliantly aggressive strategy (though that strategy played a part). The truth is that the Russian mafia caused the collapse. Soviet "reform" was nothing more than a criminal revolution. And "free elections," in a country where doctors are paid a poverty-level wage, were a boon for organized crime, which was the only available sponsor for candidates.

Today, Russian mobsters have open positions as industrialists, businessmen, entrepreneurs, and politicians, and the Russian Federation is run as mob-held territory, which explains the many well-known cases of contract killings of businessmen. These are *not* cases of inter-gang rivalry. They are executions to remind the people just who is in charge. They have helped the Mafia impose a set of unwritten rules over the entire country. If openly powerful businessmen can be publicly assassinated and no one is arrested, what happens to the average person who questions the mob?

When the leaders of the Russian Federation want to look tough on crime to appease western governments, they classify street criminals as mobsters that threaten the international community. These second-rate criminals do not come only from the criminal class. All too many are former soldiers and law enforcement officers who never found their place in the new regime. They make an easy target because they specialize in criminal enterprises like prostitution, drug trafficking, and racketeering. But more important for the West to understand is that about three hundred of Russia's criminal gangs operate internationally. Twenty-six operate in the United States.

THE RUSSIAN MAFIA IN AMERICA

Aside from assigning tasks to serving intelligence officers, the Russian mafia makes great use of the many intelligence officers who resigned after the collapse of the Soviet Union.

Many joined Russian companies that operate overseas, not knowing they were owned by the mob.

In America, the mafia relies on Russian immigrants who congregate in cities like New York, Chicago, Miami, Los Angeles, and San Francisco.

The nation's immigrant soldiers start with typical organized crime activities: prostitution and drug running. They will do anything that involves quick cash transactions. Extortion of protection money is a common tactic that works very well in immigrant communities, where people are typically afraid to go to the local police.

For legal cover, the mafia buys companies in a cash industry. Gas stations, cafeterias, and taxi companies are typical money-laundering fronts. And the Russian mafia is not adverse to cooperating with other criminal gangs.

One of their most despicable crimes is the trafficking of Russian and Ukrainian women around the world. Russian newspapers advertise high-paying jobs overseas for Russian women. While some of the women know that the offers are for prostitution, most of them believe that they will be working in exotic places away from the poverty that is now the "new democracy" of Russia.

Once they get to their new homes, their sponsors take away their passports and tell them they are to work as prostitutes. These poor women are in a land where they don't know the language and have no friends. Without their passports they cannot escape. If they refuse their orders, they are beaten and raped until they agree to do what they are told. In a recent case in the former Yugoslavia, a woman who refused to listen to her captors was publicly beheaded, as a warning to others.

The Russian mafia provides prostitutes to other criminal groups around the world. In Milan, police broke up an auction where women were being sold for an average of a thousand dollars apiece. A quick look at the Russian language papers sold in Brooklyn, New York, will disabuse anyone of the notion that Russian-run prostitution can't happen in America. I guarantee that most of the "escorts" one sees advertised—some topless—are not volunteers.

On a more frightening level is the story of how Ludwig Feinberg, a Russian mobster, purchased a Piranha-class nuclear submarine from the Russian Naval Base in Kronstadt for $5.5 million. The submarine was to be disguised as an oceanographic research vessel, but would, in fact, transport cocaine to ports in North America. To facilitate his plan, Feinberg signed a Russian admiral to a two-year contract. Feinberg was arrested in the United States on other charges, and his submarine deal collapsed. But his adventure was not much different from what already happens with the purchase of Russian military helicopters—at $1 million apiece—by the drug cartels to transport drugs.

Though most Americans don't realize it, America is already penetrated by Russian military intelligence to the extent that arms caches lie in wait for use by Russian special forces.

FBI organized crime specialists have a tough job trying to keep the Russian mafia under control. Unlike other criminal cartels, the Russian ones have a legitimate front. It is hard to stop someone—who is by all accounts the owner of a multibillion dollar legal business—from investing in America.

Mayors of the largest cities around the United States are welcoming Russian mobsters to their communities. They do not want to hear from the FBI that their new local moguls are criminals in disguise. Mayor Rudolph Guilliani of New York, for instance, enthusiastically welcomes Russian investment in his city, but his administration is apparently unconcerned about its source. The FBI is trying to stop this Russian encroachment onto U.S. soil. Only in San Francisco, however, has the FBI been successful in keeping Russian criminals out of the local economy and politics—thanks to the courage of local politicians who heeded FBI warnings and refused dirty money.

But just as in Russia, the mobsters are trying to influence not only local, but also national politics—even the president of the United States. A recent example is the case of Vadim Rabinovich and Grigori Loutchanski. Rabinovich, a Ukrainian businessman, attended a fund-raising dinner in America in September 1995, where he had his picture taken with President Clinton. This happened despite the fact that his visa had been revoked the month before and that he was known to have ties to organized crime—indeed, he had served time in prison. Nevertheless, he uses his picture with Clinton to obtain business opportunities in the Ukraine.

Grigori Loutchanski was Rabinovich's business partner in an American-based Russian commodities firm. The State Department listed the firm as being tied to organized crime and put Loutchanski on a "watch list" as a "suspected criminal." Yet, he dined with Clinton in 1993 and was given a private meeting with the president and Vice President Al Gore.

Perhaps the latest outrage that the American people have had to endure at the hands of the Russian mafia are the joint ventures between Russian and American companies. There is little question that some of these businesses are fully owned and controlled by the Russian mafia. As these joint ventures come to fruition, they will represent the most far-reaching Russian effort to enter the American economy. Even seemingly innocuous joint ventures between Russian and American companies are not immune to subjection by the Russian mafia.

Too often, American companies do not look carefully at their potential partners, and tend not to consider the consequences of their short term profits, especially when these invest- ments involve Russian bonds. Today, American investors are inadvertently supporting Russian organizations that, in turn, support terrorist countries and activities.

The most sensitive activity of the GRU is gathering intelligence on American leaders, and there is only one purpose for this intelligence: targeting information for *Spetznatz* assassination squads.

The GRU is still continuing with its traditional strategy of supporting any activity that might weaken the United States or its allies. For instance, Russian intelligence is helping Iraq subvert U.N. weapons inspections, warning the Iraqis, for example, about when "surprise" inspections will occur.

Why would Russia do this? Well, in the first place, it is anti-American. Possibly more important is the fact that Iraq owes Russia $8 billion, and therefore Russia is eager to help Iraq disguise its weapons program and get the economic sanctions against Iraq lifted. Moreover, Russian companies have signed agreements with Iraq to exploit its Qurna oil fields. Of course, these Russian companies can see the fruits of their agreements only after sanctions are lifted. Russia has very good relations with Iraq and Sadam Hussein and his government, and will do everything they can do to keep him in power.

Another problem area for the United States is Iran. As America tries to prevent Iran from getting weapons of mass destruction, Russian companies have signed agreements with Iran to cooperate on nuclear and missile technology development.

Russia and Iran have formed a joint research organization called Persepolis, which has research centers in both Iran and Russia. Persepolis provides Iran with Russian nuclear experts. Additionally, the GRU and SVR are providing Iran with technical information stolen from the West, and are training Iranian intelligence operatives.

Formal cooperation has been set up between the Baltic State Technical University (a missile training facility in St. Petersburg) and Iranian Sanam Industries Group (which is building solid-fuel, long-range missiles in Iran). According to Western intelligence agencies, five Russian institutions, including the Russian Space Agency, are helping Iran improve its missile program.

The FSB, Russia's internal security service, is coordinating visits by Iranian scientists to Russian facilities. These visits were personally approved by Vyacheslav Trubnikov, the head of the SVR. The purpose of this specific cooperation is to help Iran build their own versions of North Korea's Nodong intermediate range missiles. The Iranian versions are called Shahab-3 and Shahab-4. These Shahabs could be fielded by 1999, and are capable of hitting targets throughout the Middle East. Longer range versions of these missiles will be capable of hitting targets throughout Central and Eastern Europe. Shahabs present a very serious threat to the entire region, especially Israel. Iran, it is believed, already has chemical and biological weapons. With Russia's help, Iran will have nuclear weapons as well.

Ironically, this could eventually prove a danger to Russia, but for now Russia is interested only in Iran's money. Russian leaders did sign a security cooperation agreement with Iran on February 26, 1998, but it can't prevent a possible future attack of Russia by Iran. Coincidentally, on February 23, 1998, Russia signed an agreement with Syria to help the Syrians develop a nuclear "energy" capability. And Russia remains friendly with Moammar Khaddafi's Libya.

North Korea also presents a nuclear threat to American forces and allies. Russia helped North Korea develop its Nodong missiles, which can attack the entire South Korean peninsula. Russia has also given North Korea the technology to develop its own nuclear weapons. Russian support continues to this day to ensure North Korean armaments are state of the art, and North Korea itself has been very active in trying to sell its weapons and knowledge to other totalitarian countries.

Worse, Russian arms experts—even highly technical ones with knowledge of nuclear weapons—are often not being paid or are receiving salaries that barely keep them and their families alive. So many of them are going to "terrorist countries" and offering their services to the highest bidders. Even if they don't want to relocate to those countries, these starved scientists are willing to sell extremely sensitive information. In Russia these days, every deadly weapon is for sale.

One of the main reasons why I defected from Russia was because of the corruption running rampant throughout the government. While I was in the GRU, we had the reputation of being the "White Knight who is fighting for the Fatherland without any private interests." I was proud of that. Now the more I hear about the GRU—including its officers being involved in black market arms sales—the happier I am to have left it.

RUSSIAN BOMBS ON AMERICAN SOIL

Though most Americans don't realize it, America is already penetrated by Russian military intelligence to the extent that arms caches lie in wait for use by Russian special forces—or *Spetznatz*.

As a GRU officer, my main mission was to prepare for war. I can tell you that for the Soviet Union *and for the Russian Federation*, America was and is the main expected wartime adversary. Other countries count only as a means to attack America.

Russia remains terrified of the power of America, and Russian military intelligence does everything it can to prepare for a war that it considers inevitable. Let me be very clear about this. The GRU is still recruiting agents and is still preparing for war with the United States as we approach the supposedly peaceful, post-Cold War millennium.

Recruiting foreigners to work for the GRU is similar to recruiting agents for the old KGB or the new SVR, except the recruits have to be willing to work for Russia not only during peacetime, but also during war, when the penalty could be death. This is obviously not easy, and Americans with military information are generally hard to recruit.

Of course GRU agents don't go walking around telling potential recruits that they could face death if caught. You slowly recruit people and then figure out if they will fully cooperate with you later. It is well known to GRU operatives that many agents not only refuse to cooperate during wartime, they also turn themselves in. Along the way, they can give up everything they know.

So it is important to find motivated recruits who can operate independently. In wartime, it is often hard for GRU handlers to maintain contact and give direction. Moreover, it is important to keep a recruit away from other agents to guard against exposure from counterintelligence or from being sold out by compromised agents.

Probably the most sensitive activity of the GRU is gathering intelligence on American leaders. These people include the president, the vice president, the Speaker of the House, other congressional leaders, cabinet secretaries, and their families and friends. It also includes key military officers, and other important officials. There is only one purpose for this intelligence; it is targeting information for *Spetznatz* assassination squads.

These elite special forces are under the control of my former employer, the GRU. Some units are assigned to the Special Destinations Group. They penetrate countries shortly before a war and perform military sabotage that Americans would call terrorism. Some *Spetznatz* groups perform as assassination squads. These soldiers are familiar with all types of weapons, explosives, and mines; and they are experts at killing quickly without weapons as well. They are also trained to drive all types of military vehicles, including helicopters and small airplanes. They must be fluent in at least two foreign languages. English is the language of choice.

During wartime, they would try to assassinate as many American leaders as possible, as well as their families. They would also blow up power stations, telephone switching systems, dams, and any strategic targets that cannot be taken out with long range weapons. Especially important targets are the supposed secret landing sites for Air Force One during times of war. In wartime, the president would be aboard Air Force One constantly. While it can refuel in the air, it eventually has to land to be resupplied and serviced. *Spetznatz* forces would be expected to wait at these secret sites—which we at the GRU were responsible for finding—to take the airplane out when it lands. The use of tactical nuclear weapons would be likely. In Soviet and Russian military doctrine, nuclear weapons are not merely for deterrence; they are to be used, and *Spetznatz* has them available.

Spetznatz troops are currently training inside the United States. They regularly enter the country as foreign tourists, using fake passports and their knowledge of foreign languages to pass as Germans or Eastern Europeans.

They are the best supplied troops in the Russian military. One of the GRU's major tasks is to find drop sites for their supplies of clothes, cash, and special equipment— including even small nuclear devices, the so-called "suitcase bombs."

Popular drop sites include the Shenandoah Valley outside of Washington, D.C., and the Hudson River Valley outside of New York City. "Suitcase bombs"—nuclear weapons—could be stored in these areas and elsewhere. Russian General Alexander Lebed made international headlines when he claimed that while all strategic nuclear weapons are accounted for, there are approximately one hundred tactical nuclear weapons, identified as RA-115s (or RA-115-01s for submersible weapons), missing. That number is almost identical to the number of "strategic targets" upon which those bombs would be used. It is likely these weapons were deployed before Lebed looked into the matter. Given the contempt felt for General Lebed by many in the Russian government, it is not surprising that this information would be kept secret from him.

The media claim that RA-115s are packed into briefcases, hence the nickname "suitcase bombs." It is generally true that they can fit into a briefcase, but they usually aren't transported like that. They weigh from fifty to sixty pounds. When I was in the Military Diplomatic Academy—the GRU Training Academy—I was trained in making and camouflaging bombs of all types. I made bombs that looked like bricks, logs, rocks, and so forth. While I did not handle nuclear materials in my own training, GRU officers are trained on the general principles of handling nuclear materials, including hand-held nuclear weapons.

It is surprisingly easy to smuggle nuclear weapons into the United States. A commonly used method is for a Russian airplane to fly across the ocean on a typical reconnaissance flight. The planes will be tracked by U.S. radar, but that's not a problem. When there are no other aircraft in *visual* range, the Russian airplane will launch a small, high-tech, stealth transport missile that can slip undetected into remote areas of the country. The missiles are retrieved by GRU operatives.

Another way to get a weapon into the country is to have an "oceanographic research" submarine deliver the device— accompanied by GRU specialists—to a remote section of coastline.

Nuclear devices can also be slipped across the Mexican or Canadian borders. It is easy to get a bomb to Cuba and from there transport it to Mexico. Usually the devices are carried by a Russian intelligence officer or a trusted agent. If a Russian intelligence officer was for some reason not involved, the human missile transporting the device would be killed after safely handing it over to a GRU specialist. This is a simple security precaution.

Setting up one of these devices is complicated. The bombs need a small amount of power to keep them safely in storage. For example, the GRU specialist might have to run a very small wire to an electrical source, such as a power wire, and then attach it to the weapon. The wires can be run as far as one hundred yards or more from the weapon. The wires are small enough that they would easily break if someone tampered with them or tried to follow them to their source. In case there is a loss of power, there is a battery backup. If the battery runs low, the weapon has a transmitter that sends a coded message—either by satellite or directly—to a GRU post at a Russian embassy or consulate. The GRU would order their specialists to take care of the problem. Other problems include someone physically tampering with the device, or a basic mechanical failure.

The good news is that these weapons will not explode by accident. They automatically self-destruct the nuclear material if someone tries to tamper with the device. Also, in order for the device to explode, it must be activated, which is not a simple thing. When the nuclear bomb is to be activated, *Spetznatz* soldiers will retrieve it and take it to a safe area for initial preparation. Should the final order be given to explode the weapon, they will take it to the target, set the timer, and leave. If there is no final order, the bomb will be deactivated and returned to its drop point.

For every GRU officer, supporting *Spetznatz* assassination and bomb squads is a top priority. All GRU officers have to find at least two new drop sites a year. One day the GRU resident told me to take a "day off" and go to the Shenandoah Valley for a drive. I was told to drive down Skyline Drive, lose all tails, and take panoramic pictures of the Range View, Jeremy's Run, Stony Man, and other beautiful overlooks. Of course the weather was terrible, but the pictures did turn up some potential drop areas.

In wartime, many GRU officers—all of whom are men—would go undercover to directly aid the *Spetznatz* forces.

These wartime plans were fully in place during the Caribbean Crisis—or the Cuban Missile Crisis, as Americans refer to it—and remain fully in place today. In 1962,

Spetznatz forces were deployed all over the free world, ready to commit acts of sabotage. When no orders came to "go into action," they destroyed all evidence of their presence and went home. They were undetected and operated freely during the hottest period of the Cold War. Now, when America is less alert to the danger, think of what *Spetznatz* could do.

These assassination squads have been called into action many times around the world. During the Afghanistan War and more recently in Chechnya, they assassinated political leaders. They have also been used in the Baltic States to kill troublesome political activists. During the Reagan administration there was a standing order to target the president's defense and foreign policy advisers who were considered radically anti-Soviet, for possible "future operations."

The GRU has always been tasked with collecting information about how to make weapons of mass destruction. It was the GRU, not the KGB, for example, who recruited the rings of spies that stole the technology of the Manhattan Project.

Officially, Gorbachev killed all research into chemical, biological, and other weapons systems. Ironically, Yeltsin also had to issue a decree killing these programs years later. Recent defectors, however, tell that the research into all these programs is continuing.

One link as to why this would occur has been apparently overlooked. Back in 1979, a biological warfare research center in Sverdlovsk, now Yakaterinburg, accidently released a cloud of Anthrax into the atmosphere killing dozens of people. This incident has been well reported. However, what was not reported was that Yeltsin was the chief of the Communist

Party in that region at that time. He was responsible for the cover up of the incident, and supporters of mass destruction programs remind Yeltsin of this fact whenever they have to.

While the United States ended research into biologic warfare during the Nixon administration, research continues into antidotes to new weapons being developed by Russia and other countries that continue their own programs. Unfortunately, new discoveries by Western biotechnology and pharmaceutical firms can play into Russian biological and chemical weapons programs. These industries are heavily targeted by Russian intelligence.

The deployment of these weapons is similar to that of nuclear weapons. In the same way that Russian intelligence hides the "suitcase" nuclear weapons inside formations that look like rocks, wood, bricks, and other natural looking objects, GRU specialists can hide chemical and biological weapons. They could be brought into the country and hidden in the same ways and places.

In the GRU I was told that American intelligence had placed stores of chemical weapons near critical Russian waterways, and that they would be released killing millions of our people in time of war. I do not believe this is true. I believe the GRU was seeking justification for its own actions.

It is well within Russian military doctrine to poison water supplies to large cities. It is therefore likely that GRU specialists have placed poison supplies near the tributaries to major U.S. reservoirs.

Meteorologists, at least Russian ones, have a term, "Rose of Winds." This is the term for predictable wind and weather patterns. If *Spetznatz* and GRU agents went on war alert, they would be given dead drop sights for chemical and biological weapons, and told where to release them so they could do the most damage. One likely target would be the Potomac River, targeting the residents of Washington, DC. Small amounts of the weapons could cause minor epidemics. Large amounts could have an unimaginable deadly impact.

Another example of using intelligence knowledge of geography and climatology is the military bases in Florida. If you know the right areas, you can release toxins in the Carolinas, and during periods of heavy rain, they would be carried into the Florida water supply to kill the local population and especially the military personnel at their many bases in the state. Florida is also a major location for weapons manufacturing.

Russian weapons of mass destruction are not limited to nuclear, chemical, and biological weapons. In 1997 a Russian "scientific vessel" used laser weapons to blind U.S. pilots flying surveillance missions. The future use of this technology is to plant space-based lasers that can "blind" entire cities. Possibly they can be made more lethal.

Other instruments of destruction the Russians have had success with are seismic weapons. Spitac and other small towns in the Transcaucasus Mountains were almost destroyed during a seismic weapons test that set off an earthquake. This would have obvious applications on America's west coast and other areas of the world prone to earthquakes.

Russia has also been a leader in the development of "Electromagnetic Pulse" weapons. Basically, EMPs were identified during early nuclear testing. Scientists found that high-energy pulses destroyed electronic circuitry. Weapons based on this technology were used by the United States during Operation Desert Storm to electronically blind the Iraqis. Large scale EMP weapons can cripple cities.

Probably the most troubling set of weapons that Russians are pursuing involves the use of very, very low frequency radio signals. Early research indicates that this type of energy can be used to destroy the human brain. If they can develop a powerful enough delivery mechanism, they can kill millions of people from thousands of miles away. Another use of this technology is to influence the human brain. Russian research indicates that these radio signals—used at a nonlethal level and combined with other types of radiation—can be used to put people into a zombie-like state, and be a tool in brainwashing.

All this technology is being developed under the cover of "dual use" claims in research centers that are run by supposed civilian agencies. The GRU has been, and always will be, a major tool for use of these weapons of mass destruction, and for espionage to capture technical secrets that will make them more effective.

Still, it should not be shocking that *Spetznatz* would infiltrate America. It is simply good military practice. War is war. It sounds simple, but many Americans seem to believe that there should be a gentlemen's code, that war should be fought by soldiers in remote battlefields. Americans believe that war should be sterile, because it has never hit their home soil since the Civil War of 130 years ago, and even then, only in the southeastern part of the country. Russia has been rampaged for centuries by every would-be world conqueror. Millions of Russians have died on their homeland during wars. This is a feeling that Americans do not know. The only way you get an enemy to submit is by bringing the war to his people. Maybe if the United States had been willing to bring the Gulf War directly to the Iraqi people, Saddam Hussein would not be in power today. But America, apparently, has different interests. American special forces are taught to perform rescue operations. This is not a military mission for Russian special forces. Instead, *Spetznatz* train terrorists; something American special forces won't do.

The GRU has always believed that any activities that help to disrupt Western countries—countries that are still considered Russia's enemies—are good for Russia. Therefore, the support and sponsorship of terrorist actions is more than justified for the GRU. Before the collapse of the Soviet Union, terrorist training came out of the GRU budget and was performed by the *Spetznatz* assassination squads. Who better to train terrorists then people trained to be terrorists? And yes, the world has seen this training in action. The Aum Shinrykyo cult in Japan, who planted gas bombs in Tokyo's subway, was a star pupil. Like other groups, the cult paid the GRU for its training. Most of the Arab terrorist groups were also trained by *Spetznatz*. Even the terrorist group that sponsored the World Trade Center bombing had been trained by people who themselves had been trained by the GRU.

I guess it might be more honorable to assume that the GRU was performing this training to protect the Russian homeland. However, in the early 1990s, the GRU decided that it would train any terrorist group that was able to pay for it. If they are politically aligned with Russia, all the better. However that is not a requirement. And that, too, is why I left the GRU. But before I go into that, perhaps I should tell you a bit more about myself, how I was trained, and what I did in the service of the GRU. It is often instructive to see the world through the eyes of one's enemy.

Chapter 2

MY MILITARY CHILDHOOD

MY EARLIEST MEMORY is of looking out my window as a self-propelled artillery gun turned onto my street. The gun was part of the frequent parades held on holidays commemorating the Bolshevik Revolution. I lived in Leningrad, near Smolninsky Park, and I was excited at being right on the parade route. I was three years old at the time, waving my little red flag as high as I could so that all the soldiers would see me. And like all of my neighbors, I cried out, "Long life to the Red Army," as the guns, tanks, and soldiers went by.

I was probably more enthusiastic than most, because I felt the cheers were also for my father, a lieutenant colonel in the army. Being the son of a war hero was extremely prestigious in the Soviet Union. My father was an example to all Russians, but mostly to boys and teenagers. I was proud of his medals, especially the gold and red stripes he wore, indicating the serious wounds he had received during the wars in which he had fought. To me they were a sign of courage. To him, they were a reminder to keep me out of the military.

I was born in 1946 after my father returned from the Second World War, badly wounded but not a cripple. My father had fought and been wounded in five wars, but he never thought of leaving the military. Nevertheless, the military decided to transfer him out of the service to the Ministry of State Security, or the MGB, a precursor to the KGB, with a higher salary and many more privileges.

He was chosen in part because of his record of loyalty and service, which had included guarding Vladimir Lenin, a fact that later also helped me get into a prestigious military training academy.

Like all of my neighbors, I cried out, "Long life to the Red Army," as the guns, tanks, and soldiers went by.

Shortly after being transferred to the MGB, my father was sent to Moscow to work in the Kremlin. In 1949 he was sent to Karaganda, a small city in Kazakhstan, where he served in the MGB headquarters for Central Asia. His specific job was with the "reeducation camps" that dealt with people who opposed the Communist regime. My father never talked about his job, but he obviously didn't like it. In fact, a year later he applied for early retirement—just two years short of when he would have received his full pension and benefits.

The next year, we settled in Sochi, a resort city on the Black Sea coast. This area was reserved for people who were carefully screened by the MGB, because Stalin's dacha (or resort) was located nearby. This dacha is now Yeltsin's primary Black Sea retreat.

As I grew up, I dreamed of serving in the military but my father did his best to paint the military as unattractively as possible. He wanted desperately to keep me from entering the military, and to that end tried to find me other interests, including piano lessons, which I hated. After a few lessons, I realized that learning the piano would not help my dreams of being a war hero and protecting the Motherland, so I began to cut them and go to the beach instead.

I lived about ten minutes away from the coast and the "wild beaches" that were too rocky for the tourists and most locals. Swimming, I told myself, was much more important for my future career in the military. I spent hours in the water every day. My friends and I would swim until we turned blue with cold. But we would always take time out to play border guards, pretending to protect our Motherland from the fascists and, later, from the American invaders.

We would play border guards, pretending to protect our Motherland from the fascists and later from the American invaders.

It was in the early 1950s that the face of our enemy changed from the Nazis to the imperialistic Americans. Everything that we saw or read helped to buttress our belief that Americans were evil, and would invade our Motherland at the very first opportunity. The Soviet press worked overtime on news stories and movies that recounted the latest atrocity committed by American soldiers around the world.

At the time, my favorite movie was *A Mistake of Corporal Zbruev*, in which an army corporal didn't report being sexually seduced by a beautiful American woman. He was eventually blackmailed by diabolical American spies. His army commander and various Soviet counterintelligence agents were the heroes of the movie. My friends and I memorized almost every line of the film. We all wanted to be in the army, and fought to be the counterintelligence officers when we would reenact scenes from the movie.

During this time, I led a carefree life. But one day I saw my father marching toward me on the beach, and I knew my honeymoon with the sea was over. A fisherman had told on me. My father was terribly disappointed because I had lied to him by skipping my piano lessons. But he would have been even more disappointed had he known that my time at the beach was spent preparing for the military, and playing spy-catcher. For me, what hurt most was not the whipping, but that I had disappointed my father. I had the privilege of being his son, and I had failed him.

> **Our belief was that Americans were evil, and would invade our Motherland at the very first opportunity.**

I had no such feelings about my mother. When I was seven, a few weeks before beginning elementary school, my father took me for a two week cruise on the Black Sea. When I returned, my mother was gone. She had run off with a naval officer. It happened so quickly that it made me numb. During the divorce process, a judge asked me if I wanted to live with my father or my mother. I told him that I wanted to live with them both, together. That was impossible, and the judge gave custody to my father. It was that simple.

At the age of ten, I became infatuated with another movie, *Scarlet Shoulder Straps*, about the elite Suvorov Military School, which was named after the famous eighteenth-century field commander Generalissimo Alexander

Suvorov. In the early 1940s the school was opened to the sons of Soviet military officers who served in the Second World War.

Students at the Suvorov School lived in military barracks, just like the army. It was not the academic regime that gripped me, but the military and physical training. Students also received special language training, which meant that I could begin the job of becoming a counterintelligence officer. Not only that, I could wear a special all-black military uniform with scarlet stripes. The special dress uniforms were even more impressive.

To a Soviet ten-year-old, the military was something like a cult that you had to belong to. Besides, my father had remarried. And so I asked my father about joining the Suvorov Military School. He threw up every possible objection, but in the end he agreed. Boys, however, could join the school only after completing the fourth grade, and with the highest marks. And so, in due course, I graduated from fourth grade with the highest marks in the class. My father was both proud of my accomplishment and deeply unhappy at what it meant.

In the summer of 1957 my father and I traveled five hundred miles through the mountains of the Northern Caucasus to the Suvorov Military School in Ordzhonikidze (now Vladikavkaz), at that time the capital of the Northern Ossetia Autonomous Republic. I was getting exactly what I wanted, and my father was getting exactly what he didn't want: a son who was following in his footsteps.

Chapter 3

AMERICA, THE ENEMY

I SPENT EXACTLY seven years inside the walls of the Caucasus Suvorov Military School, where I turned from a boy into a man. Here, I had my first kiss, made lifelong friends and enemies, and enjoyed real books. Books became a lifelong passion and would help me establish the necessary rapport to help me recruit spies years later. It was there where I learned to prepare for war, came face to face with it, and luckily learned to respect it.

The life was hard—hours upon hours of classes and homework, and harsh physical and military training in merciless weather. We endured the bitter cold and often felt we were starving to death. I lived this life from age eleven to seventeen.

When I was thirteen, I was called into my commander's office and told that my father had died. I was devastated—my father was the only family I had known, and I idolized him. But I had to be a good soldier, and so I didn't show my grief.

My father's funeral in Moscow was a true hero's funeral, held in the main hall of KGB headquarters, an honor reserved for very few people. I was proud, but my life would never be the same.

When I got to my home in Sochi, the local police chief came and told me that my stepmother didn't want me in the house anymore. My real mother heard about it and asked me to stay with her and her new family. The whole situation was like a dream. My home in Sochi was the only thing I had left in my life, and it was being taken away from me. I am truly grateful to my mother for allowing me to stay with her during all my home leaves. And, besides, she introduced me to Natalie, my wife, for which I can never thank her enough.

Lieutenant Colonel Yakushev, our instructor for military translation and interpretation, told us that the United States was *The Enemy*.

As I said earlier, the Ordzhonikidze Suvorov Military School was commissioned in the early 1940s. But earlier, it had served as a fortress for the Russian empire and later for the Soviet Union in the Northern Caucasus. In the 1920s the Vladikavkaz Infantry Academy was founded on these same grounds and became one of the most famous in the Soviet Union. In the early 1940s, almost all of the students from the school were killed, but they stopped the Nazis from taking over the Transcauscasus region.

In order to graduate, we had to receive a diploma in military mountaineering. We spent a couple of weeks in the cold mountains with full packs on some of the hardest mountains the ranges had to offer.

Our regular military training was not so difficult, and great fun for a teenager. We spent thousands of hours learning how to use weapons of all types, from kitchen knives to tanks. We learned how to fire revolvers, mortars, artillery guns, and we could fire our AK and AKM rifles in any condition, from any position, day or night, with marksman ratings. Not bad for a bunch of teenagers.

We also trained in military planning and procedures and played war games. We drove trucks, cars, armored personnel carriers, tanks, and any other vehicle the military had to offer. We did all of this, of course, in order to fight our biggest enemy. Lieutenant Colonel Yakushev, our instructor for military translation and interpretation, told us that the United States was *The Enemy*. Yakushev spoke English well, and there were rumors that he had worked in intelligence until he made a mistake and was sent to our school. I took one of his admonitions with me for the rest of my career:

> *Put these words in your ass, and remember them. You can have enemies among your classmates or on the streets, but not in the military. In peacetime, there are potential adversaries. During war, you have an adversary and you need to respect and to understand him so that you can beat him. Don't forget it. And now you need to learn how the American military is organized, because if you capture an American soldier and you feel he's lying while you are interrogating him, ask him the structure of a military unit. If you know it well, you'll also know if he is lying. Then you can use other methods of interrogation.*

At the top of our daily dose of propaganda was America's aggressive imperialism, whose goal was world domination, pure and simple. But we were ready to take on America in any future war.

I was sixteen years old when this American imperialism became very real to us during the Caribbean Crisis. One night, we were woken up—not by the usual trumpet blast—in the pitch dark. Our company commander arrived in our barracks in his full combat uniform, pistol and all. The platoon commanders and master sergeant accompanied him, all dressed for battle. They woke us by touching our shoulders. It was unusual and scary. They then told us to get up quietly, and dress for battle. We put on our uniforms and ran to the weapons depot where we picked up our machine guns, anti-tank weapons, grenade launchers, and ammunition.

We went outside and formed into platoons in total darkness. Then our platoon commanders ordered us to leave the school and hike into the mountains, where we would meet in the caves. Half of us were to carry the platoon's ammunition, the other half were to go to the location of the first- and second-year students. I was assigned to that group. Each of the cadets in my group was assigned to take care of two or three of the young students and make sure they made it safely up the mountains.

At sixteen, I had been assigned my own youngsters to take care of. In the darkness, I found my three charges, who were eleven and twelve years old. I told them there wasn't anything to worry about, but they felt better when they recognized me in the dark. I checked their weapons, ammunition, and rations, and then we all marched into the mountains. For the first five miles, my boys were all right, and they looked like little, but real, soldiers. I was very proud of them.

A little later we left the highway and the road became difficult. When I saw that one of my boys was tiring, I took his pack and rifle and carried them myself. By the time we reached the valley between the Bold and the Long Mountains, I was carrying my equipment as well as that of all of my charges.

When we reached what we called the Emergency Point of Concentration, I left my boys in care of their company commanders. I was very proud of them for making it all the way up the mountains. Our location was deep inside the mountains. Our commander explained that Soviet forces were on combat alert and were being moved from their peacetime location to their reserve areas because the Caribbean Crisis could develop into an all-out war between the United States and the USSR.

At the top of our daily dose of propaganda was America's aggressive imperialism, whose goal was world domination, pure and simple.

The first thing we had to do before sunrise was to reach a valley and establish camouflage nets over our location. We were to limit our movements and be ready for a nuclear attack. American battleships were moving into position around Cuba, and the Soviet missile forces were preparing for a retaliatory or preventive strike against the United States and its allies. We therefore had to be inside our bunkers until we received special orders from the supreme commander. We were told that if anyone was outside the bunkers and saw a nuclear blast, he was to jump into the bunker immediately. The bunkers were dug into the sides of mountains and were covered by metal and concrete.

We spent all our time listening to our platoon commander's portable radio, using our knowledge of physics to make speakers that increased the volume. We heard about the negotiations between Khrushchev and Kennedy and their attempts to resolve the crisis—all, of course, from the Soviet perspective, which put full responsibility for this situation on the Americans.

According to Soviet radio, the incident had been orchestrated in Washington, and was an American provocation. The destruction of the world was being prevented only by the strong countermeasures of the Soviet government. Not a word was mentioned about the nuclear missiles in Cuba. This was divulged to the population only after it had become common knowledge in the West.

But to my knowledge, the entire truth about the Caribbean Crisis is still not known by the American public. My own information about the crisis came later, when I was in the GRU Training Academy, where I made a full analysis of the operation, code-named ANADYIR.

There was much more to the Caribbean Crisis than ever came out publicly in the Soviet Union. Colonel Mescheryakov, a GRU officer who would later become a three star general and the first GRU deputy chief, helped organize the large-scale movement of Soviet troops into Cuba. Between July and October 1962, more than 42,000 Soviet troops were relocated to the "Island of Freedom," as we referred to Cuba. Included was a missile division. This division had more than 150 nuclear warheads, which were loaded on strategic missiles that could reach anywhere in the United States. There were also tactical nuclear weapons that could have taken out all of the U.S. naval ships that were blockading Cuba.

The GRU helped orchestrate the disinformation campaign to keep these troop movements a secret, with some support from the KGB. This operation, for obvious reasons, was a tightly held secret. For example, in the Ministry for Foreign Affairs, only Minister Gromyko was informed about the operation. The extent of the disinformation campaign was far reaching. To cover the movements of two thousand of the troops, a story was planted that one of the USSR's largest cruise ships was making a first-ever trip to Cuba. But all of the passengers were military officers traveling in civilian clothes.

Khrushchev himself was involved in the disinformation campaign, insisting until October 25 that there were no nuclear missiles in Cuba, even though the Americans were well aware of the facts. As a side note to history, even Fidel Castro was not informed until 1992 about the total number of missiles in Cuba. Nor did the U.S. government know until then about the tactical nuclear weapons that were there as well.

By Soviet general staff estimates, Operation ANADYIR was successful. There was no American attack, but more important, after the Soviet missiles were returned to the USSR, American nuclear weapons were secretly removed from Turkey. These latter weapons could cover the entire European portions of the Soviet Union, and presented a grave threat. Kennedy was allowed to keep their removal a secret so that he could save face.

All of these details became known to me years later, but during the Crisis we believed the official explanation of the Kremlin. We were still in school, and we were safe. In our eyes, our country saved us from the American imperialists. We were hiding from American nuclear weapons, and we were living through evidence of American aggression. I became more resolved than ever to join the military and help protect my country.

At the end of the second day in the bunkers, we were informed that we could return to our school, although still on alert status.

In a few hours, we were back in our barracks and back to our normal life. But my classmates and I would never forget those two days of living with the real possibility of nuclear war, a war more cruel than all previous wars put together. The lessons of the Caribbean Crisis were ingrained in our minds.

I studied everything about the United States and its military with infinite care. I wanted to know everything about its weapons, structure, culture, history, and conflicts. I began to follow closely all American political events, because nobody ever knew what those crazy Yankees would do next. In short, I needed to protect my Motherland.

With the image of the United States as an unpredictable and aggressive political and military adversary stamped on my mind, I graduated from the Suvorov Military School in 1964. I decided to stay in the army and continue my military education at the regular military academy in Tashkent.

Chapter 4

TACTICS AND STRATEGY

IN 1964 TASHKENT WAS THE CAPITAL of the Uzbek Soviet Socialist Republic. Tashkent was technically in Central Asia, and it was incredibly different from anything I had ever seen before. The city was hot and dry, pockmarked with canals, and the odors of Asian spices cooking in restaurants and homes permeated the streets.

I arrived by train with Senya and Yura, two of my classmates from the Suvorov Military School. Senya was from the Rostov-Don section of Russia. Yura was a Jewish fellow from Crimea, who preferred to be identified as a Crimean Greek. Life in the Soviet Union was difficult for Jewish people, but Yura was a loyal Soviet citizen and wanted to serve his Motherland.

During my three years at the Tashkent Joint Arms High Command Military Academy, I was trained to become a platoon, company, and battalion commander. And I dreamed of going on to attend the Frunze Academy in Moscow, the only place you could learn to command regiments and divisions, and then on to the Soviet General Staff Academy, where I would learn to command corps and field armies.

During our intensive training, we spent about 60 percent of our time studying military plans and procedures relative to tactics and strategy, most of which focused on the United States. Our instructors kept reminding us that the Americans were our top enemy, and becoming stronger and more aggressive every day. War with the United States was inevitable, and had been held off thus far only by virtue of our strong and intelligent Soviet leadership.

> **We spent about 60 percent of our time studying military plans and procedures relative to tactics and strategy, most of which focused on the United States.**

Physical training and the martial arts were also a major part of our curriculum. Only about 30 percent of our time was given to traditional academic subjects, mostly science. I excelled in math and was offered the opportunity to transfer to a university in Moscow, but the only thing I wanted was to protect my country by being a better soldier.

Ten percent of our education was in Marxist-Leninist ideology. Success in this subject was considered proof of your loyalty to the Communist Party and the Soviet government, and was crucial to a future military career.

The whole class spent two months each year serving as platoon and company commanders for real military units. My most memorable command was serving as a platoon commander in a motorized infantry regiment on the Edge of the

World, the only real way to describe Takhta-Bazaar in Turkmenistan.

I made the two-day, thousand-mile train trip to the edge of the world with about a dozen of my classmates. We spent several hours in Mari, the administrative district of the area, which looked like a picture from the seventeenth century, with sheep and horses in the streets. The only buildings that were not made out of grass were the local KGB offices and the Communist Party headquarters.

From this ancient town we took a train to Takhta-Bazaar. When our train arrived, we saw two yurts (Asian nomad tents), and a huge mud pit—replete with pigs, sheep, and camels trying to keep cool in the desert heat. Behind this pit was a mile-long, ten-foot-high concrete wall, with the traditional red stars on both sides of the gate. This was the entire town of Takhta-Bazaar. Technically, there were 2,200 people in the town, 2,190 of whom were military personnel assigned to the infantry regiment.

Our nearest neighbors were at a guard post on the Afghanistan border about thirty miles away. Division headquarters was in Kushka, about fifty miles across the desert.

Only a few of the two hundred officers had their families with them. Most wives, after a few months, would pack up and go elsewhere—anywhere else would do.

Four people had apparently tried to desert from the base a long time ago. Three of them died in the desert. One reached Afghanistan, but the border guards returned him to the regiment. The only problem was that his head was missing. Nobody tried to desert after that.

Another discouragement to deserters was that Takhta-Bazaar was considered to be the snake capital of the world—the area was infested with hundreds of different types of snakes. After a time, we lost our fear of all the snakes but one. Cobras and other dangerous snakes give a hissing warning, but not the gurza snakes. They would not only attack without warning, but would sometimes wait for someone to walk past and then attack from behind.

War with the United States was inevitable, and had been held off thus far only by virtue of our strong and intelligent Soviet leadership.

After almost three months my classmates and I were happy to return to Tashkent, with its paved streets, solid buildings, and movie theaters. But my luck didn't last for long. Soon after our return, I woke up in the middle of the night to find my bed shaking and moving. The Tashkent earthquake came on suddenly. At first we didn't know what was going on, but then we heard an order pierce the dark.

"Earthquake, everyone out of the building!"

We swiftly became soldiers again. We grabbed our clothes, backpacks, and rifles and began to run outside. But on the bunk next to me, my neighbor was sitting on his bed repeating a single phrase, "Don't panic, everything is okay. Don't panic, everything is okay."

Yura, my Jewish friend, yelled, "He can't move, let's take him out!" Together, we carried him to the window and jumped out.

We took refuge in the safest place, the academy stadium, but others were not that lucky. All of the newer homes and buildings in the area were totally destroyed. Under the debris were thousands of bodies of men, women, and children. We saw this destruction the next morning when we were ordered into the town to secure the area, help rescue workers, and stop criminals and looters. It was the only time in my life I was given the order to shoot without warning.

I was numb as I helped to collect and organize the dead bodies. I kept telling myself that I had to be strong in the face of death to help provide order, while all around children were crying for their dead parents and parents were crying for their dead children. I felt the pain of people who searched vainly for their loved ones, who most likely were dead. All I could think was that I was a soldier and I had to act like one so that Soviet citizens could feel their government was helping them. Inside though, I was fighting to hold back the tears.

Everyone in my class was astonished when we heard Moscow radio report that only four people had been killed in the earthquake. I had personally helped line up hundreds of dead bodies, and knew that there were thousands more. Later the reported number of deaths increased, but only slightly. Our instructors told us that this disinformation campaign was to avoid international assistance for the disaster victims. Tashkent was a "closed" city, and international relief would mean that foreign spies would infiltrate our country with the real relief workers. This was an ominous precursor of all the other things that I would one day learn were lies.

"We can and will restore Tashkent by ourselves," was the official Soviet position, and we and the real victims didn't have any choice but to accept it.

Since it came during exams, the graduating class was not called away when there was an uprising in Chimkent, a city near Tashkent. The population had rebelled against their corrupt officials, who frequently put people in jail without a trial. But two nongraduating companies took part in "restoring order," assisting the local police and some airborne units to break up demonstrations and arrest the activists.

My schoolmates were not overly careful in their use of force. They were allowed to arrest and shoot people without warning. The officials in Chimkent and the Uzbekistan Communist Party chief, Sharaf Rashidov (later officially recognized as a criminal of the state because of mafia connections), were of course happy about this performance. So when Moscow considered shutting down the Tashkent Academy, Rashidov personally asked Soviet leader Leonid Brezhnev one question, "If you close the academy in Tashkent, who will protect socialism in central Asia?"

There was no more talk about closing the school.

It was 1967, and the Six Day War began just before we graduated, provoked, we were told, by the United States. Our academy was put on alert until Israel won the war several days later. In private, we of course condemned Israel as a pawn of the United States, echoing the official Soviet line. But privately, we, the future leaders of the Soviet military, admired and studied the Israeli campaign and the strategy used by General Moshe Dayan.

Within a few days, Israel reached the Suez Canal, destroying the Egyptian army, which was armed with Soviet weapons. The Israelis then proceeded to take the Golan

Heights from Syria and the Gaza Strip from Jordan. We found this incredibly exciting.

Around June 1967, rumors started circulating within the Soviet military that Moshe Dayan was a Soviet general and a "Hero of World War Two." Stalin himself had specifically allowed Dayan to emigrate to Israel to help the infant nation because Stalin thought that Israel would provide a counterweight to American and British influence in the region. But then the Soviets began to back the Arab nations. One of my instructors told me privately something that I will always remember: "We did everything right and spent billions of dollars for weapons for our friends and allies in the Middle East. We only made one small mistake, we chose the wrong allies."

The next month, the whole class finally graduated with the rank of lieutenant and waited for our new assignments— the better your grades, the better your assignment.

I was assigned to the Tank Division in the Southern Group of the Soviet Forces in Hungary, along with one of my classmates, Senya. Yura, my Jewish friend, was an excellent student, but was sent to the Far East Military District, a most undesirable post in the middle of nowhere. The living conditions there were very harsh, and the likeliness of a promotion for Yura was very small.

Chapter 5

HUNGARY: LEARNING TO PENETRATE ENEMY LINES

ON THE TRAIN RIDE to Hungary, some of the shortcomings of the Soviet Union became quickly apparent. Right at the point where the train crossed from Ukraine to Hungary, things became "cleaner." Before crossing the border, open fields were filled with trash. There were hills of garbage and mountains of coal, sand, and other construction materials. Fields grew wild. But after the Ukrainian town of Chop, fields were clean, construction materials were in closed warehouses, and fields were well kept. In Hungary, the local people seemed to care about their homeland.

This was my first time outside the Soviet Union, and I thought that life would be terrible. But then, of course, Hungary was a Soviet ally, and was probably much better off than the rest of the world. What else would a young lieutenant think? The posters denouncing the Soviet occupation were disheartening, however.

After a four-hour train ride, I and about a dozen of my classmates from Tashkent arrived in Budapest. We were met by a Soviet military patrol, which took us in a passenger truck to the headquarters of the Southern Group of the Soviet Armed Forces, located in the Budapest suburbs, where we received our assignments. Our group slowly dissipated, and I stood alone with Senya. He had been one of my best friends for over a decade, and now we were being separated. He was sent to the Thirteenth Tank Division in Central Hungary, and I was going to the Nineteenth Tank Division in the town of Estergom in northern Hungary.

The Hungarians hadn't lost their taste for life even after more than twenty years of communist rule.

When I arrived in Estergom, a military patrol took me to division headquarters. I was told to get back on the train to Budapest, but to get off halfway at Pilishchaba, which literally translates to "Half a mountain, half a hole," headquarters of the 119th Separated Reconnaissance Battalion with a Deep Reconnaissance Company.

Pilishchaba was located in a beautiful valley of the Karpaty Mountain Range, surrounded by woods and trees. Nobody met me at the station, but when I went behind it I saw an old bus without wheels, set on concrete blocks. A sign on the top said in Russian, "Blue Danube River Restaurant."

Sitting at this makeshift bar were four Soviet junior and senior lieutenants. After a few drinks, my new associates helped me carry my luggage to the battalion headquarters about two miles away. My new home was a series of old buildings behind a wire fence, originally built by the Nazis during the Second World War as a prison camp.

I spent four of my best years at this base. I was assigned to the Deep Reconnaissance Company, which was divided into two platoons; one of the platoons had two groups and the other had three. Our main mission was to be able to fight independently and penetrate enemy lines. From there we were to function in the "Deep Rear" of our adversaries; perform reconnaissance; capture and interrogate POWs; destroy or capture enemy headquarters and nuclear weapons; and capture and hold important bridges, tunnels, and mountain crossings until the regular troops arrived. This type of mission would qualify us as Special Operations forces in the West, but in the Soviet military we were limited to penetrating only one hundred miles. The *Spetznatz* forces were supposed to operate beyond that limit. They were operational units; we were only tactical units.

I knew that I was moving into an exciting new phase of my life, where I could serve the Motherland while at the same time serving my family.

My first job was to retrain my group—good soldiers with good basic skills but badly trained—in special tactics. We spent weeks going through different scenarios, learning how to move quickly and quietly, and so on—the skills I myself had learned in Suvorov school and Tashkent academy.

The *Spetznatz* groups were organized similarly, but they had better equipment—better and lighter weapons, special clothes with electrical heaters built in, individual radios, and much more. One of their most notable privileges was their high-calorie rations. Supposedly my unit would get the same equipment during a real war, but I had my doubts. Still, while their equipment was superior, I didn't think their training was any better.

I was able to confirm my feelings on several occasions. The first time was in the spring of 1968 when our company took part in a reconnaissance exercise and the *Spetznatz* forces were our adversaries. Our mission was to locate our adversary's missile launchers. A helicopter dropped us into our area of operation, and we performed our reconnaissance over a dozen square miles using a search pattern, as I had taught. Finally, one of my men reported that he spotted something unusual.

I checked out the situation and found that a *Spetznatz* soldier was trying to do the same thing we were, but not as carefully. I had taught my men to move through the woods quickly and quietly. By following the "enemy" soldier's movement we were able to locate the other people in his group, all of whom we captured. I was pleased when someone from the Southern Group of the Soviet Armed Forces Intelligence Directorate ordered me to detail in writing how the capture had been accomplished.

Probably as a result of this and other successes, the deputy chief of the Intelligence Directorate approached me with a business proposal. He wanted me to join the *Spetznatz*, and after a little training and special preparation, I could see a real operational battlefield in Southeast Asia. It was the beginning of 1971, and everyone knew what "Southeast Asia" really meant. It was clear that he was referring to Vietnam, although that was officially a secret.

Joining *Spetznatz* would have given me a brighter military career, but by that time I had other plans. I told this senior intelligence officer that I had applied to the Lenin Military Political Academy Law School, and that my application had been approved by the Political Directorate and a special commission in the Military Political Academy. I was scheduled to take the entrance exams in two months.

"Okay, let's make a deal," my would-be recruiter told me. "If you pass the tests, go and good luck to you. But if you fail, call me at this telephone number. By the way, why is a person like you looking at law school, anyway? Especially with your knowledge and experience in the reconnaissance business?"

I tried to explain it to him, but it wasn't easy. He finally accepted my politically correct answer, that I wanted to assist our future leaders in fighting crime, and especially crime in the military. My real reasons, of course, were quite different.

By this time, I was married to Natalie. We were married during my last home leave, and she moved to Hungary to be with me. She was pregnant with my first, and my only, child. And I wanted to spend a long time with my family, in good locations—an impossibility if I went into the *Spetznatz*.

Another strong reason for going to law school was that I was starting to lose all my idealistic views about the military. I had put in four years in the regular military and had seen what the real world was like. I worked hard and didn't have any free time of my own.

Most of the other officers spent their free time at the Blue Danube River Restaurant playing cards and drinking. I wasn't opposed to drinking in the good company of friends, but I preferred to do it over a good meal. Unfortunately, there was only one restaurant and it was five miles away.

I loved Hungary and its people. The Hungarians hadn't lost their taste for life even after more than twenty years of communist rule. And they still worked hard, as their mothers and fathers had before them. But the Hungarians didn't like the Soviets, whom they looked upon as military occupants of their country. There were frequent reminders of this. The most common place was in public restrooms, where the bathroom graffiti frequently read, "Russians go home!"

Even though we were close to Budapest, I saw it only a few times. You had to have special permission from the battalion commander to leave the immediate area, and it was seldom granted. The living conditions for officers was better than that of the enlisted people, but not much. Married officers had a ten- by fifteen-foot room for themselves and their families, and we shared a kitchen and bathroom with a dozen other families. My salary was enough for minimal food and clothes, and we could think about buying a simple radio or tape recorder. But only senior officers could afford larger items like TV sets and washing machines.

I also had to put up with the corruption of senior officers. My battalion commander would illegally sell some of our supplies to local merchants and assign some of our troops to work with military equipment for other merchants. They, of course, would receive payment for the work of the soldiers.

I tried working hard, but I really didn't see a future in my career. I actually progressed quickly, to senior lieutenant and then to captain, and was named commander of the Deep Reconnaissance Company. But it was obvious that the best I could hope for in the regular military was to be a battalion or regiment commander, at a remote garrison.

A job in military justice would be different. The offices of Military Prosecutors or Military Tribunals were usually located in big cities. Prosecutors, judges, and investigators also had much better living conditions and better salaries.

When I reached my threshold of endurance, I began to study for the entrance exams. I took the test in June 1971 at the Central Training Center in Khaimashker. The exams lasted two weeks, and during this time I was informed that I was a father—my daughter, was born, and I was overjoyed. I knew that I was moving into an exciting new phase of my life, where I could serve the Motherland while at the same time serving my family.

At the end of July, I was told that I had passed the exams and was being transferred to the Soviet Army Main Political Directorate so I could attend law school. I was given the customary one month home leave, which Natalie and I spent in Sochi with her parents.

At the end of August, I reported to the Lenin Military Political Academy to attend its law school. The other schools at the academy trained high-ranking military political officers or political commissars for the Soviet armed forces, the KGB, and MVD, and for the armies of the Warsaw Pact countries. It was a very prestigious academy, and I couldn't have been happier.

Chapter 6

MILITARY JUSTICE

AT THE MILITARY POLITICAL ACADEMY, we spent a great deal of time studying Marxist-Leninist ideology, the history of the Communist Party, political economics, and the philosophy and theory of scientific communism. This academy was a cornerstone of communist ideology in the Soviet armed forces, and total loyalty to the communist regime was demanded of all students. At first I thought that this would not be a problem.

But as it turned out, I lost my ideological virginity in the walls of this fortress of communism, paradoxically because of the privileges I had as a student there. I was allowed to visit the closed archives of the Central State Lenin Library, and to view many original documents that had handwritten notes and the signatures of Lenin, Bukharin, Sverdlov, and other communist leaders. As I read their notes, it became obvious that not only were these people not saints, as depicted in Soviet history books, but many of them were mentally and morally deranged. They had ordered the deaths of millions of ordinary persons whose only crime was their dissatisfaction with the political ambitions of Soviet leaders. I was horrified when I read a paper signed by Lenin, ordering intelligence officers to go into small towns and stir up civilian uprisings— after which the military would arrive and kill everyone in sight. After my research, I no longer believed in communist dogmas and principles. I was sickened by the sight of the pervasive huge portraits of Lenin and other Soviet leaders, with their hypocritical and psychopathic smiles. Everything that I had been taught was sacred was a lie. But I couldn't give up everything I had learned. I still managed to believe that socialism was fundamentally sound and good for the people of the Soviet Union. Everything wrong with the country was laid, by me, at the feet of the corrupt and egomaniac leaders. I also did this, in part, because personally I was happy and enjoying law school. My grades were very good, and I was optimistic about my future in military justice.

This academy was a cornerstone of communist ideology in the Soviet armed forces, and total loyalty to the communist regime was demanded of all students.

But in the middle of my last year, my class commander, a middle-aged colonel, called me into his office and introduced me to a gray-haired man in his forties in civilian clothes. He was introduced to me as Sergei Fedorovich. My class commander told me that I could speak as freely with Sergei as I did with him, and then he left me alone with this smiling, gray-haired man.

"Tell me briefly about your background, please," he said. After about five minutes, he asked me several other innocuous questions in rapid succession.

"What do you think about the American war in Vietnam? How many miles are there between Moscow and Vladivostock? What do you know about U.S. military capabilities? What NATO countries do you know? Who were your grandparents on your mother's and father's sides? What did you see at Gorki Street between Manyezh Square and Maykovsky Square? What is the highest mountain? What is the deepest place in the ocean?" And so on.

I lost my ideological virginity in the walls of this fortress of communism....

I had no problem with any of his questions, except one. "What punishments did you incur in your previous military experiences?"

I gave him my "faults" as listed in my official personnel file, but I could see that he wasn't satisfied. So I decided to tell him something that was not in my file, but which he seemed to know anyhow.

"And one more fault. I was under arrest for three days at the Budapest military guardhouse for fighting with other officers."

"Reason?" he said brusquely.

I told him about a party at which three officers from another battalion got into a fight with a friend of mine. By the time I noticed, my friend was on the floor being kicked by all three of them. I went over and stopped them—I actually had to knock all of them unconscious. When my friend regained consciousness, he jumped on one of his attackers, knocked him to the ground, and pounded his face. I pulled my friend off of him, and we walked away.

The next day, the wife of the officer that my friend had pounded complained to my battalion commander. She said that I had used my combat martial arts to attack him. I told my commander that if I had, all three of them would probably be dead. He agreed, but said that he had to do something, and that it would be a good thing if I were to disappear for a few days in the military jail. I didn't mind, as it was a chance to catch up on some reading. He also promised that he wouldn't include the incident in my personnel files.

My former commander must have broken his promise and put it in the secret files that commanders keep on people. I was not allowed to see those files, but apparently this strange civilian was. Now he just smiled and said that he probably would have done the same thing.

> **It became obvious that not only were communist leaders not saints, as depicted in Soviet history books, but many of them were mentally and morally deranged.**

After that, Sergei asked me a few more questions and said we would probably be talking again. Two weeks later we met, and he asked me, "Have you ever heard about the Glavnoye Razvedyvatelnoe Upravlenie, or the GRU, of the Soviet General Staff?"

After I said yes, he frowned and immediately said, "Please identify the concrete sources of your knowledge!" I told him about some Top Secret field reconnaissance training documents that I had used during my training at the

Reconnaissance Battalion. The credit for writing the document was given to the GRU.

Sergei relaxed once again and then introduced himself as a colonel in the GRU who was looking for recruits for the Soviet Military Intelligence Agency. He asked me if I would like to join the GRU, assuming that the GRU Recruitment Commission thought that I qualified.

I said that I thought myself lucky to have the opportunity—and I wasn't lying. Although I had already changed my career by going to law school, and was satisfied with it, I still thought of myself as a reconnaissance man. Returning to my original plans, at a higher operational level, was exciting.

I also enjoyed the image of being a "spy," with its surrounding aura of romance, mystery, and danger. This image had been cultivated by the books I had read and the movies I had seen.

After I gave my answer, Sergei asked me to sign a paper saying that I would never disclose that I had talked to anyone from the agency or cooperated in any way. I signed the document in a heartbeat, and then Sergei gave me a bunch of forms to complete by our next meeting.

For the next month, I continued my studies while completing dozens of pages of the application. In the beginning of the spring of 1975, I was informed that my application had passed the first phase and that I now had to take special tests at a GRU location. There were hundreds of different questions, with a tight time limit, but I had no difficulties doing it.

A couple of weeks later, I was in front of a table facing one- and two-star generals. They informed me that my test results were acceptable, and asked me dozens of questions about everything under the sun. At the end of the grilling, a two-star air force general introduced himself as the chairman of the Recruitment Commission and welcomed me to "the Family of Soviet Military Intelligence."

An army colonel, who served as a secretary for the commission, later instructed me that after I graduated from law school and had my home leave, I was to report to the GRU Main Training Center, called the Military Diplomatic Academy (MDA). There, I would receive my future assignment.

At the end of July, I graduated with honors. When in due course I arrived at the MDA, the officer on duty did something odd. He tore my name off the list of visitors. I asked him why, and he told me it was none of my business. I never again walked through the main gates of the Military Diplomatic Academy.

At 10:00 AM, all freshman in the MDA met in the main hall of the academy. I was told that I was assigned to the First Faculty, which meant that I was to work undercover as a real spy.

My new boss, Army Colonel Yudgin Zhuchin, announced that students from the First Faculty would be issued civilian clothes. Nobody was ever again to see us in a military uniform. We were also forbidden from using the front entrance of the MDA headquarters, but to use the rear entrance stuck between some apartment buildings.

We were also told that the next morning we were to report to the entrance of the Music Band complex of the Moscow Military District on Komsomolsky Avenue, where we would spend the first year of our new education. Out of the hundred people that started with me, only fifty would complete the course.

Chapter 7

TRAINING AND TERRORISM

ON SEPTEMBER 1, 1975, I stepped through the gates of the Moscow Military District's Music Band compound, one of the best protected bands in the world. I walked through the heavy metal gates by showing the guards an ID badge with my picture and pictures of small birds, alligators, and other animals. Other people had pictures of dogs, cats, and so forth (the position and type of animals changed on a monthly basis and were used as a form of identification). We had these silly pictures, but no names. My name became nonexistent the moment I stepped through those ugly gates.

This fortress-like building, the GRU First Faculty, was a small part of the GRU's training facilities and the site of our first year of training. As new recruits in the First Faculty, we received a quick introduction to the intelligence world. Every one of my new classmates was a captain, major, or lieutenant colonel. Now, in our civvies, we looked like mid-level bureaucrats.

At our first meeting we sat around talking for a few minutes until Colonel Zhuchin came in and gave us the formal, "Welcome to the GRU" talk. The first thing he gave us was our assignments to our training groups. These groups were divided by operational areas and were permanent. They were not to be discussed.

Group One was assigned the United States. Groups Two and Three would target Europe. Groups Four and Five would target Africa and Arabian countries. And Group Six, my assignment, would target East Asia. I was positive that I would be assigned to the United States or possibly the European groups, since I knew English fairly well. Besides, I would never look Asian. But orders were orders.

> **We studied the American armed forces. We learned the structure of the U.S. military from the lowliest private to the president, as well as a detailed description of every weapon.**

We then heard the new, and obvious, rules: don't tell anyone, except your wife, that you are in any way affiliated with the GRU; hide your uniforms; report any strange occurrences; and on and on. They could just as easily have told us to keep our mouths shut.

Our wives attended their own meeting and were told basically the same things, but they also received some support for entering a mysterious life they did not choose.

The next item was our names. We were not to use our last names anymore. From this point on, we were to refer to each other by a three-digit number. Outside the building we could use our last names when we were not being associated with the GRU. This was supposed to minimize the risk of an operative going bad and knowing the names of all the other trainees. Of course, this was ridiculous; we all knew each other's names, and we joked about it. The situation became more ridiculous the following year when the GRU realized that the numbering system wasn't working. So they told us to start using our wives' maiden names instead. Now not only did we know each other's last names, we knew information about each other's wives as well.

Colonel Zhuchin named covert operations instructors for each of the operational groups. We were told only their first names and that they all held the rank of colonel.

When the meeting broke up, we went to our group classrooms on the third floor. It was here that I met all of my classmates for the first time. Our student commander was Nickolai, a naval lieutenant commander and a senior officer in a nuclear missile submarine in the Northern Fleet. He resigned after the first year, because he missed the power that came with his former position. Another student, Victor, became and remained my best friend until my last days as a GRU operative; he was a captain from the Strategic Missile Forces in Siberia. He eventually received the USSR's highest military awards.

The GRU and the KGB helped to fund just about every antiwar movement and organization in America and abroad.

I was assigned to the Chinese subgroup, along with Fedor, an army captain. He was assassinated in the mid-1980s in Pakistan after he had been promoted to military attaché. According to GRU rumors, he was killed by the CIA because of his success in recruiting Americans. When, after I defected, I talked to the CIA about this, I was told that they too had investigated his death and found he was killed by a lunatic.

Several members of our group dropped out quickly. One was surprisingly naive and left because he didn't want to recruit spies. Another left because he couldn't learn his assigned language. Another was caught in a KGB counterintelligence sting (the KGB used one of his neighbors to get him to disclose that he was assigned to the GRU). Others were caught talking about their GRU training outside of the MDA. Some decided to leave their wives, and divorce was considered a security risk in the GRU. Still others were caught having "unauthorized relations"—or adultery, in the civilian vernacular—which was also considered an unacceptable security risk. Then there were trainees found drunk in public. And so on. GRU recruits were held to an incredibly high moral standard.

> The GRU had a larger budget for antiwar propaganda in the United States than it did for economic and military support of the Vietnamese.

At our first meeting we were also introduced to our primary instructor, or "baby sitter," as we called him. Igor Sergeevich told us that he was extremely proud to be assigned to our group, because we had the highest IQs of all of the officers in the class. We needed it to learn Chinese and Japanese. China was our #2 enemy, second only to the United States, and an extremely strong adversary. Of course this warmed our souls, but I learned to curse my assignment as I studied long and late to learn the crazy Chinese characters. We had to speak like natives, and were left with little room for failure.

Our most important subject was "Special Preparation and Training," learning the theoretical and practical aspects of meeting and recruiting citizens of countries and "friendly foreigners." We had to know how to find people, develop them as contacts, get them to cooperate with the GRU; and learn how to handle recruited agents and "trusted persons," and how to evaluate the information they provided. We also, obviously, had to become experts about our targeted countries.

During the latter part of our training, we were given operational assignments. Each of us was given the name of an organization in Moscow to target. We were to establish contacts and develop relationships to gain information that was just on the edge of being illegal. But if our agents proposed anything actually illegal, we were to report it to our commanders immediately.

My target was the Law Literature Publishing House located near the Kurski railway station. I spent all of my evenings hanging around people I generally tried to avoid— the homeless, drifters, thieves, and other such types. But I quickly found a small cafeteria that was used as a hangout by the publishing house employees on Fridays. I then decided on my first collection target—the USSR Criminal Code, which was not for general sale in the Soviet Union.

In a few days, I established contact with a low-level worker there and I finally talked him into selling me the criminal code. This was probably the most important lesson of my life, because it taught me the psychology behind recruiting informants—that is, how to manipulate people.

As part of training, we practiced secure and safe meetings, as well as the risky ones with recruited agents. We practiced dead drops, secret signals, and other types of spy craft. In the laboratories, we practiced making dead drop covers. We would take rocks, cans, bricks, or logs, and hollow them out so we could hide information inside them. We also had to find places to place dead drops. Each of us had to find a new dead drop, with only two rules: don't steal the ideas of your classmates, and don't put your dead drop on the dirt or concrete. The reason for the last rule? In Western countries, people keep their property and their neighborhoods clean; something we didn't normally think about in the Soviet Union. In the Soviet Union, trash provided camouflage. In the West, it would be cleared away.

In the labs, we practiced making explosive devices out of objects that were used for the dead drops. We used timers and radio signals and beams to detonate them. We practiced writing hidden messages with microfilms and microdots. We also practiced using regular film that would destroy the picture if it wasn't developed in the right way. And of course we had our little spy gadgets with hidden compartments. Our toys included cameras, pens, necktie holders, and cigarette lighters.

Electronic bugging devices took a year of our time. We learned all about listening devices that would collect information and store it. They would then upload the information to a passing satellite. There was also the modification of electrical lines that allowed television sets to be used as listening devices. We also became adept at countersurveillance technologies and techniques. We learned not only to detect them, but also to confuse and confound them. And much more.

In our second year, we were taught to avoid surveillance. KGB operatives would try to track us when we went on undercover missions. This was actually the most fun of all our training. Typically, students would perform their mission and report how successful they were. Almost always, their boss would look at a file, start laughing, and tell them in detail everything that they had done, including what they had eaten.

This happened to me only once, and it was my fault for not understanding Chinese as well as I should have. I was meeting with an agent, who was really a GRU lieutenant colonel. He tried to tell me in Chinese that there was something strange with our meeting place, and I didn't catch the subtle hints he was trying to give me, so I missed the surveillance. This was an incredibly valuable lesson for me. In China in 1983, this lesson saved my life and that of my agent.

Although most Westerners don't realize it, the GRU is one of the primary instructors of terrorists worldwide.

For over a year, we studied the American armed forces. We learned the structure of the U.S. military from the lowliest private to the president, as well as a detailed description of every weapon. Then came the American "special services" like the FBI, CIA, DIA (Defense Intelligence Agency), NSA (National Security Agency), and so on. We were taught their structures, traditions, locations, missions, methods, successes, and mistakes.

Only in our second year did we learn about our operational target's military. In my case, it was the Chinese People's Liberation Army and Special Services. This was while the United States was pulling out of Vietnam. We spent a great deal of time studying the Vietnam War, which was considered a Vietnamese victory over American imperialism. While the GRU instructors would not state it directly, they strongly implied that the GRU was responsible for the Vietnamese success. The GRU had a massive presence in both North and South Vietnam; their operatives worked under the cover of the North Vietnamese Special Services.

Our instructors also told us about how the GRU influenced the American public. The GRU and the KGB helped to fund just about every antiwar movement and organization in America and abroad. Funding was provided via undercover operatives or front organizations. These would fund another group that in turn would fund student organizations. The GRU also helped Vietnam organize its propaganda campaigns as a whole.

What will be a great surprise to the American people is that the GRU and KGB had a larger budget for antiwar propaganda in the United States than it did for economic and military support of the Vietnamese. The antiwar propaganda cost the GRU more than $1 billion, but as history shows, it was a hugely successful campaign and well worth the cost. The antiwar sentiment created an incredible momentum that greatly weakened the U.S. military.

But our instructors kept stressing that just because the Americans lost did not mean they were in total decline.

America, they said, was becoming much more aggressive and a danger to civilization because it would have to reassert itself as a world power and avenge its defeat. For this reason, no matter who or what our targets, we were always to prioritize America.

Our instructors told us that to obtain an agent from our targeted countries was good, but to get an agent from America was great. Targeting Americans was extremely difficult because of their loyalty to their country and their fear of the FBI and other U.S. counterintelligence agencies. But the GRU was quite successful at recruiting Americans who lived abroad. Once they returned home, however, only a few would continue to cooperate. We would lose 90 percent of our American agents this way.

It goes without saying that overtraining included refining our knowledge of Marxist-Leninist ideology. We were members of the Communist Party, and furthering our knowledge demonstrated our loyalty. But compared to the Military Political Academy, our lessons in ideological education were minimal, and happily so. There is only so much propaganda even a loyal Soviet can take.

We were also considered military officers, and were expected to be ready to command large military units, such as divisions, corps, or field armies, if necessary. Our military education was intended to be the same as what we would have received from the Military General Staff Academy.

I don't know why our heads didn't explode with this plethora of information. But we were rewarded with certain privileges. The one that stands out was that we were not required to help the local collective farms harvest their crops, as I had had to do at my previous training academies—two months of back-breaking work in all kinds of weather.

Instead of going to farms, we were sent to the GRU dacha, or training center, at Istra Lake—twenty-five miles outside Moscow. We went there about one weekend a month. During World War II, this dacha was used as a training center for Soviet military "illegals." These people would sneak into the target country and take on the identity of regular citizens. They would then perform their regular intelligence assignments. The center was later used as a training center for "the fighters for the national liberation movements"— more appropriately called international terrorists.

Although most Westerners don't realize it, the GRU is one of the primary instructors of terrorists worldwide. The Communist Party Central Committee specifically authorized the GRU to train terrorists in order to further the USSR's political goals and support its allies. After all, what could be better than to have other people commit terrorist actions that further your own goals?

There was also the GRU Special Center for the training of terrorists at GRU headquarters. The KGB provided financial and communications support to terrorists, but the operational training and support was reserved for the GRU. The GRU has trained terrorists from almost every country in the world, including Iraq, Libya, Iran, Egypt, Syria, Lebanon, Palestine, Italy, Germany, Spain, Turkey, and Latin America. Where no terrorist groups existed in countries inimical to the USSR, the GRU would help to form them, and then provide them the necessary training, funding, and organizational support. So, for example, while the terrorists involved in the World Trade Center bombing may never have attended GRU training, the GRU was responsible for the formation of the terrorist group that they belonged to.

Of special note: the GRU helped train the Aum Shinrykyo cult of Japan, which launched the gas attack in the Tokyo subway. The GRU has also been involved in terrorist actions such as murders in Israel, Italy, France, Turkey, Pakistan, and other lands friendly to the United States. And again, the World Trade Center bombing shows how this activity can reach into the United States itself.

There are training facilities all over the former Soviet Union, but most of them are located in the southern part, such as the old Odessa Infantry Training Academy, because Arab and Latin American terrorists do not like cold weather.

Supposedly, Gorbachev ordered a halt to terrorist training under pressure from Western countries. But this training continues not only for political factions, but for any group willing to pay for the service. The GRU is also willing to set up special training facilities outside the former Soviet Union for those.

Every evening at the dacha, we had a party, which our "baby sitters" of course attended. They believed that if we could not function normally here, we would be useless in like foreign situations. Ironically, being a heavy drinker was a benefit, because you could be effective while everyone else was drunk.

One example of how this served me well was in China, when I was drinking with a Chinese diplomat at a cocktail party. After two or three drinks, he started to talk about his work and seemed to forget that I was a Soviet. And because

I knew how to keep my head, I remembered everything he was saying and steered the conversation into even more sensitive subjects.

During the first year of training, we had some "secret" parties—parties without our baby sitters—which would include everyone from our operations and study groups. But we soon learned that some of the private topics we spoke about at the parties became known to our baby sitters. They in turn would report the information to Colonel Zhuchin. And thus several comments made privately at our parties led to people being expelled from the MDA. More important, we became suspicious that some of our fellow recruits were providing information directly to Zhuchin. Later we also thought that the wife of one of our friends was providing information to the KGB counterintelligence officers assigned to the MDA. These KGB moles were searching out traitors in our group, and we always feared that they would create one to justify their presence. So my friends and I started to perform our own counterintelligence operations.

As a result, we started having much smaller and more private parties. We developed our own little cliques, and these turned into some of the strongest friendships in our lives. I hope these friends of mine are still doing well. But I won't name them, because I don't want them to get into trouble as a result of their friendship with me, especially if they are still in the GRU.

The three years at the MDA flew by, and in 1978, I graduated as top student in my group, although because of a silly mistake I failed to win honors. I also missed our graduation party, because I had to leave for Singapore for my first operational assignment. Singapore had expelled two GRU officers as spies, and the GRU field office needed two replacements who knew Chinese and were not registered by any country's counterintelligence departments as intelligence operatives. The operational cover, or "roof" as we called it, was that we were students taking part in an international exchange program. This limited the assignment to one year, but it gave the GRU time to train other people who could be more specially suited to the assignment. Vitali and I were selected for this "extremely important mission," as it was phrased in our assignment letter.

Being the first people in the class to be given operational assignments carried some benefits. Vitali and I were the first people to be given our own personal apartments in Moscow—the dream of every Soviet military officer. If I had to leave Natalie for a whole year, I was much more comfortable knowing she was being taken care of while I was gone.

By American standards, our apartment was on the slum side—a one-room apartment with a two hundred-square-foot living room, a tiny kitchen, and bathroom. But to us, this was our slice of heaven.

When I got to the international airport in Moscow, I was truly impressed. It was clean and orderly, and the duty free shops were stocked with items that ordinary Soviets could never hope to find. These shops were also supposed to be reserved for foreigners. This airport was far from representing the real Moscow lifestyle, as the propagandists were trying to imply. For me, it was among the first lessons about the outside world.

By the time Vitali and I took our seats on the plane, I saw that the other students were already drinking. We soon noticed that many of them were wearing slightly better clothes and had more expensive vodka than the others, and we realized that they were actually KGB officers. This was our first experience with our "neighbors," as we called them.

Our group consisted of twenty-four people, most of whom were pretending to be from universities. We were introduced to each other a couple of days before at the Ministry for Higher Education, where we signed papers acknowledging the responsibilities of Soviet citizens traveling abroad. I was introduced as a student from Leningrad State University who was working on a masters dissertation on the Chinese language. Vitali was from the Far East University.

A Ministry official appointed a leader of our group and a deputy. The leader was a "clean" student, a fellow who was really working on his doctoral research. But the deputy, I soon learned, was a KGB captain from the Tashkent territorial KGB office, under the cover of language instructor at Tashkent University. His Chinese was only at the level of a second year student at the MDA, and I must admit that this warmed my heart.

By my count, there were only six real students in our group and fifteen KGB officers. Later my suspicions were confirmed. After several months in Singapore, the KGB officers lost their facade of superiority and became normal young men. Vitali and I became friends with many of them. Unfortunately, some of them later met with tragic deaths.

All in all, it was a very exciting day for me, because it was my first trip to a real foreign country. Hungary was nothing compared to the exotic Orient.

Chapter 8

SINGAPORE

A FEW PROBLEMS during our trip to Singapore were more serious than a bunch of drunken KGB officers. We were victims of typical Soviet bureaucracy. When we arrived in Singapore, no Aeroflot officials were there to meet us. We arrived at the airport in the early evening, but didn't leave it until late that night, because of various bureaucratic delays that humbled our sense of self-importance as "elite GRU operatives," but that gave us more time to marvel at the consumer splendor of the Singapore airport. By the time we were cleared to go, it was too late to take us to Nanyang University, where we would be living. So they took us to the embassy, where we spent the night on chairs and sofas in the reception hall. Our problem with sleeping was not only our makeshift beds, but our KGB associates. They started drinking, singing, and dancing the minute the embassy officials left us.

That night our "neighbors" became totally drunk, broke a mirror in the bathroom, and threw up on some expensive carpets in the visitor facilities. We later heard that the KGB station chief investigated the incident, but since he could not find a non-KGB scapegoat, he gave his people a verbal reprimand and that was the end of it.

During the drive from Singapore City to Nanyang University was when I saw proof of what the propagandists have always said about capitalism. Out of the windows of the bus I saw houses made from cardboard down the street from palatial estates. This was my proof that capitalism lived at the expense of the poor as I was always taught. At Nanyang University, twenty-five miles from Singapore, we were given language placement tests. I was assigned to Chinese 2-2, which translated to the second year, second semester of Chinese language and history. In the class besides me, there were two clean students and a KGB officer from the Tashkent field office. There were also two Japanese men, Amato and Okhara, and three Americans, Shirley, Brian, and Chris. What surprised me most about the Americans was that they knew so little about the Soviet Union, supposedly their most vicious enemy. They only seemed to know that Siberia was a very cold place. And they were startled by my knowledge of America and its literature, since I had consumed the novels of Mark Twain, Jack London, Theodore Dreiser, Ernest Hemingway, and many more.

> **What surprised me most about the Americans was that they knew so little about the Soviet Union, supposedly their most vicious enemy.**

At the end of the first week, the Soviet students had to report to the Soviet Embassy for a so-called "Trade Union Meeting," during which the KGB and GRU agents reported to their field offices while the clean students watched movies or did translation jobs for the embassy.

When I reported to the GRU field office, the acting resident was navy Captain Victorov—his cover, Soviet Trade Mission representative. He was in shock after the recent expulsion of the other two GRU officers, and expected to be expelled himself at any time. He claimed that he was under twenty-four hour surveillance and could not do anything outside the embassy.

He also claimed that the recent problems were a result of increased counterintelligence activities throughout Southeast Asia. After the Vietnam War, the Soviet Union was trying to replace American influence in the region. Local governments, however, were trying to protect their sovereignty against communist agents, and in consequence had beefed up their counterintelligence activities. Additionally, Vietnamese incursions into Cambodia were widely believed to be supported by Moscow. The other countries in the area were afraid that they would be next.

We were going into a dense jungle filled with snakes and a variety of other hazards... we would step on something strange and slimy, but we went on, convinced of our courage.

Captain Victorov told Vitali and me that we were not to recruit anyone, but to establish basic contacts and provide the field office with general support. This meant that we spent our weekends writing cables about the operational situation in Singapore, and spent the rest of the week making contacts and doing our academic work at Nanyang University.

Our life for the next few weeks was simple and uneventful, but this didn't last for long. Colonel Yuri Ivanovich soon took over from Captain Victorov as GRU resident. At our first meeting he asked us: "You guys have been here for a whole month. Where are your recruits?"

It is impossible to recruit anyone that quickly. We explained that we had been told to stay away from the local people, and he immediately rescinded all previous instructions and ordered us to provide him with names of possible recruits within two months.

He also told us that by the next weekend, he wanted us to tell him the missile targets of the Singapore Air Defense Missile Battery. This military base was located in the jungle a few miles from Nanyang University. In addition, we were to continue writing our radio cables, which were considered valuable by GRU headquarters.

Finally, we were to establish contact with American naval personnel. The aircraft carrier the USS Enterprise was going to arrive in Singapore within the next couple of weeks, and its crew was our target. Every GRU and KGB officer in Singapore was going to be trawling for recruits.

We decided to concentrate first on how to get the missile battery information, since we only had a week to do it. We felt proud that we were going to perform a dangerous assignment. After all, we were going into a dense jungle filled with snakes and a variety of other hazards. Vitali and I put on our winter boots for protection and bravely entered the jungle behind the university sports complex. We saw monkeys and snakes, and were covered with mosquito bites. Every so often, we would step on something strange and slimy, but we went on, convinced of our courage.

Our courage quickly changed to embarrassment when we saw a young boy sleeping peacefully under a tree that was filled with snakes. When he heard our steps, he woke up. We pointed to the snakes, warning him of the danger. He told us only cobras were poisonous, and they wouldn't attack you unless you touched them. Then he added, "Are you looking for the missile battery?"

We were stunned. He told us he had run into another university student, a "red-haired man" (local slang for a European), who was looking for it the previous day. The boy offered to show us the way. It was three hundred yards behind a nearby hill.

When we got over the hill, we found the missile launchers, pointing in different directions, but not toward Malaysia or the straits.

When we got back to the dormitory, we were met by André, a KGB lieutenant pretending to be a student from Leningrad State University. He watched us come out of the jungle and grinned widely.

"Hi, guys, how was the jungle? I was there yesterday, and didn't have much fun with the mosquitoes. But for your information only, you can see the missile battery from the roof of the library."

In shock, we went to the roof of the library, which didn't have any mosquitoes or snakes, but comfortable benches and a soft ocean breeze. The view of the missile battery was beautiful.

We then had to prepare for the arrival of the *USS Enterprise*. The regular GRU and KGB officers were assigned specific restaurants, bars, clubs, and other social spots to recruit sailors. As university students, we were to search out contacts at concerts, in the streets, and at other inexpensive places visited by lower-ranking sailors.

Vitali and I were assigned with two KGB officers to go to a gala concert of local rock music bands. When I arrived at the theater, I fully expected to recruit most of the Americans that I met. Again, I needed a dose of reality.

It was impossible even to think about recruiting people. In the first place, you could not tell who were the undercover police officers and who were the counterintelligence officers. Dozens of people were obviously trying to infiltrate the crowd to maintain order and watch for illegal activity.

Next, when I did strike up a conversation with Americans, they asked the obvious question, "Where are you from?" When I told them I was from the Soviet Union, they stopped the conversation dead.

The only thing I got from the *USS Enterprise* was a headache. I soon learned that none of the other officers had had any success either.

While I was still looking for local residents to recruit I discovered something that I didn't like. One of the KGB officers, Nickolai, was making friends with people in the university Reserve Officers Training Course (ROTC). The local counterintelligence officers noticed this as well. As a result, Nickolai was under almost constant surveillance, and so I had to avoid him or come under the watchful eyes of the local counterintelligence officials as well.

To satisfy the field office, I tried to recruit people at the university. The best I can say was that I made many friends, but nothing more.

My first real operational accomplishment was quite unexpected. It happened just before Christmas, when I was looking for a stereo to send home as a Christmas present. Being on a limited budget, I had to find a relatively inexpensive one.

I found a good JVC stereo at a small electronics store on Orchard Street in the downtown area of Singapore. There was one in the window, and the store manager, Lamar, offered to sell it to me, but I said that I wanted a new one. Lamar told me he was from India and went on to say that he would order me a new stereo from the factory in Japan. He implied that he could get "anything" produced in Japan. I asked him to order the stereo.

When I next met with Colonel Ivanovich, I asked him what the GRU needed from Japan. He looked at me strangely and said, "What do you mean, from Japan?"

A week later, he gave me a list fifty pages long. Every line was a different item with a price we were willing to pay for it. All of these items were to be sent to GRU headquarters. The United States had export restrictions on many high-technology devices to the Soviet Union, and the USSR used various means to bypass them and buy the stuff legally and illegally; illegally was usually cheaper.

Before I left his office, he also told me about three microchips that were extremely sensitive, and said that they would go for between $3,000 and $5,000. He told me to be very careful about my negotiations with Lamar, because it would be difficult to explain how a student with a $300-per-month salary could afford these things.

But to Lamar, business was business, and he didn't ask any questions. He also got the microchips for a much cheaper price than I was told to expect. The deal was done. I gave him my money for my stereo, and the GRU's money for the microchips, and in due course the chips were sent to GRU headquarters via diplomatic pouch. We later got a message from Moscow confirming the value and importance of the chips. I was also given a request to buy some American electronics devices used for naval navigational systems. Lamar got me these items as well.

I visited Lamar often, but only when I was sure I was not under surveillance. At the time, Singapore wasn't very crowded, so it was easy to spot people tailing you when you changed buses, doubled back, and so on. Drug dealers, moreover, were becoming more prevalent, which diverted some of the attention of the counterintelligence agencies.

Step by step, I increased the level of sensitivity of the items that I asked Lamar to get. Of course, I gave Lamar larger commissions as well. He didn't seem to care at all where the money was coming from.

As my time in Singapore drew to a close, I was instructed to transfer Lamar to an incoming GRU officer. I had already listed Lamar as a "Trusted Person" and a possible agent.

Lamar was able to expand his business with the GRU money, and did not hesitate to accept my replacement. As far as I know, Lamar is still providing the GRU with restricted electronics and is likely extremely wealthy by now.

Vitali and I returned to Moscow and our families. When we arrived at GRU headquarters, we were told that we would get our next operational assignments after our home leave. We had plenty of time and money saved up to go anywhere, and we decided to spend some time at the GRU resort at the Black Sea near Abkhazia's capitol. It is now in ruins because of the war in Georgia, but in 1979 it was a beautiful resort.

While we were at the spa, I got a cable from Moscow telling me that I was promoted to major in recognition of my success in Singapore. After that I looked forward to getting my next assignment, but I was disappointed.

My next operational trip was to be to China, as I expected, but first, I had to go to the mysterious First GRU Subdirectorate. Why? Because I would be under the cover of a TASS correspondent, and I had to spend at least a year learning to be a foreign correspondent.

For a military commander to become a journalist was something of an insult, or at least a let-down. I couldn't know, of course, that this would be one of the most rewarding parts of my career. My articles would run on the front pages of newspapers and magazines throughout the Soviet Union, and I was proud to learn that my name would become popular with military correspondents all over the world. But first I had to learn a whole new career.

Chapter 9

LEARNING THE CRAFT

WHEN I GOT BACK TO MOSCOW, I reported to the mysterious First GRU Subdirectorate. This was a lot easier said than done. Few people knew the location of this office. I was told to go to the Metro station at People's National Guard Street, then to a furniture store near the station and call a number from a public phone in the store. An officer from the subdirectorate would come and get me. And so he did.

This extremely elite unit was, and still is, located behind that furniture store on the first two floors of an apartment building. The nickname for this office is the name of the furniture store. To get into the building, you walked in the front door, used the intercom, and were let through a heavy metal second door. Inside, there was a security guard from the Ministry of Defense Security Brigade. After a short ID check, you went to the officer on duty. He would examine your papers and ID again, and then tell you where to go.

I was told to report to a corner office. There I found three desks and my new boss, Colonel Igor Sergeev, who welcomed me to the unit. His group consisted of all undercover officers of the TASS and Novosty News agencies, the Soviet government institutions connected with the movie industry, and student exchanges.

Colonel Sergeev told me about the other people who shared his office. One was responsible for all GRU agents assigned to the Foreign Ministry. The other oversaw the officers working for Aeroflot, Morflot (the Soviet merchant marine), Fisheries officials, and the Ministry of Atomic Energy. People in other rooms were responsible for overseeing officers assigned to Foreign Trade and other ministries, state committees, and institutions with people who were in regular contact with foreigners.

I was assigned to Group Zero... all of the meetings were held secretly, so nobody would know who my real employer was.

There were twenty-five operational groups. Commanders and deputies for each of the groups gave out assignments and acted as intermediaries between the operational groups and the other GRU main elements.

The main task of the First Subdirectorate was to establish contact with foreigners who were living in or visiting the Soviet Union. The purpose: possible recruitment. Part of the job was to establish contact with Soviet citizens who might know a foreigner. The First Subdirectorate also provided the GRU Information Directorates with support. I helped with the orientation of certain officers to the GRU or the retraining of those working undercover in other areas.

Members of the First Subdirectorate were the only military officers allowed to have any contact with foreigners inside the USSR. If any military person was caught with foreigners, they would be severely punished. The First Subdirectorate was responsible for 50 percent of all collection by the GRU, and considered the most elite. As a result, the First Subdirectorate was subordinate directly to the GRU Director, General Ivashutin. The First Subdirectorate chief served as his representative to the Military Industrial Commission.

This Commission had regular monthly meetings that were chaired by the Communist Party general secretary or the Soviet government prime minister. The heads of all Soviet ministries and state committees would attend these meetings, along with the heads of companies involved with the military-industrial complex. This was their opportunity to request information or work from the KGB and GRU. But they also, of course, had to provide funding for their requests. These requests went into the Annual Tasking Document that was the collection bible for all KGB and GRU officers. The document was distributed throughout the world, and listed all of the items that were wanted by the Soviet government.

Colonel Sergeev told me that I was assigned to Group Zero. My immediate commander was Colonel Vavilov, who worked in TASS as the senior European editor. I was given his office and home telephone numbers, and told to meet with him as soon as possible. Before leaving the "furniture store," I handed over my military ID card, and was given a civilian passport and another ID card, which had those silly little MDA-type animals on it.

When I arrived at TASS headquarters in downtown Moscow, I went to the security desk and called Vavilov. He came down and led me to the personnel office. An hour later, I had a TASS ID portfolio that looked very official. It had a hard cover case, with the official Soviet symbol on it, and a card signed by the TASS editor in chief. I also had a letter introducing me to the editor in charge of the TASS Reporters Editorial Section, where I was to learn my new trade.

It was a full-time job, but I had to make time every day to meet with Colonel Vavilov, and to report to Colonel Sergeev as well. All of these meetings had to be held secretly, so nobody would know who my real employer was. I became a TASS junior editor in the Reporters Editorial Section.

My new coworkers were friendly, but from time to time they seemed worried about me. Apparently my resumé indicated to them that I was not a "clean" reporter. I told them that I had attended Leningrad State University and Nanyang University, that I had worked at PROGRESS Publishing House in Moscow, and that I had no high-ranking relatives. My "cover" resumé was good enough to fool foreigners, but Soviets knew better.

They knew that to move from Leningrad to Moscow without the help of high-ranking relatives or special government dispensation was almost impossible. They also knew that at least 60 percent of TASS reporters abroad and 30 percent of reporters at headquarters were with the intelligence services. Since they didn't know whether I was from the KGB or GRU, they assumed that I was from the KGB, and the KGB was responsible for all internal counterintelligence work. So everyone spoke very carefully around me.

I was soon introduced to my future partner, a well-known journalist named Leonid Shevtsov. He taught me my new profession. He sent me to the Pushkin Art Museum to cover an opening of an Indian art show. I attended this ridiculous event and rushed back to TASS to write my story. Leonid noticed my frustration and said something I never forgot: "If you don't do it, nobody will, and then we will all be in trouble. So just do it, good or bad. We have plenty of editors who can correct your work."

I don't remember how many times I had to rewrite that damn story, but by the time it was accepted, I hated every word. But it was accepted.

In a few months, I considered myself a real reporter, but I soon discovered how wrong I was when I was transferred to the Socialist Countries Section, which included China.

Ilya Maslennikov was my new editor and a member of the TASS Colloquium, which was a big honor. He didn't say a word to me after I handed in my first story, but his deputy, Sergei Frolkin, told me to forget everything that I had learned and to write articles his way. I really didn't have a choice.

My work at the Chinese Desk was much more useful for my real job. I got to read the Chinese newspapers and magazines and to see everything coming out of the Chinese Information Agency, Xinhua. I could also read intelligence reports on China that were classified as "Secret" by the Soviet Union and forbidden to ordinary Soviet citizens.

My formal journalism training lasted about a year, although in reality, it would last my whole life. In the spring of 1980 the Communist Party Central Committee reviewed my file. Members of the Propaganda Department (in charge of TASS) and the Administration Department (in charge of the GRU), examined me and sent me on to the Central Committee Deputy secretary. After telling me about his intelligence experience in Europe for twenty minutes, he showed me the door and said, "Good luck."

This time, I was able to take my wife and daughter with me. On our direct flight to Beijing on an Aeroflot IL-62, we were the only ones in the economy section, designed for two hundred people. The reason was the open hostility between China and the USSR. After a recent border confrontation, the USSR was declared "the main enemy of the Chinese people," and Moscow responded in kind.

We arrived in China on May 15, 1980.

Chapter 10

CHINA

WHEN WE ARRIVED, we found the Chinese people were not so full of anti-Soviet hate as we had been led to believe. In fact, the local officials were friendly, and we had no problem leaving the airport's restricted areas. My only problem was that I soon learned there were many more Chinese dialects than I thought possible. I knew I was going to have to study harder, because as I learned at the MDA, subtle modifications in wording could mean life or death for me and my agents.

At the airport, we were greeted by the TASS bureau chief, Arthur Blinov—actually a lieutenant colonel with the KGB. This was his second station abroad. Previously, he had been a roving Southeast Asian correspondent. Later, in the United States, he was a reporter for *Izvestia*, and later an official SVR liason officer.

Riding from the Shoudu airport with my family, Arthur told us about our new home. On the drive into town, Arthur pointed out some incredibly small, gray, one-story buildings, typical Chinese homes. They had no indoor plumbing or electricity. And they were the lucky people, we were told. The unlucky ones had no roofs.

We passed mile after mile of these tiny homes, until Natalie got fed up and asked when we would reach the center of the city. Arthur told us that this *was* the center of the city and that we would be at the embassy in a couple of minutes.

Unlike Singapore, there were no large, handsome, modern buildings. Beijing's "cultural revolutions" had crushed any technological progress. This was the gray, barren capital of a militaristic society that threatened my homeland.

Yet I fell in love with this city after I got to know its streets, lanes, and people, whom I found to be hard-working, friendly, and totally unpretentious. They always seemed to be themselves, no matter what the situation. It was refreshing to learn that the smallest good thing would give them great joy in their otherwise cruel existence.

The embassy was a grand compound, almost fifty acres in total size, that was built when relations between China and the USSR were excellent. We put our luggage in our new "apartment"—a room with two beds and a separate kitchen and bath. Unfortunately, it also had roaches, bugs, flies, and many other things that I tried to forget about.

Arthur invited us to dinner at the Chinese restaurant in the Minzu Hotel, which catered to foreigners. All the TASS reporters and their families were there to celebrate our arrival. I was introduced to Evgeni Verlin, the only clean TASS correspondent in the country, and met Gennadi Krisheev, who was a KGB captain under TASS cover and would become my best friend in China.

We had a wonderful time, but Gennadi preferred "real" Chinese restaurants. The following day he took Natalie and me to one of his favorites, situated in the downtown area frequented by the locals. To say it was dirty would be a gross understatement. There were cigarette butts, pieces of paper, and food all over the floor. Added to this were a couple of emaciated cats, who fought the rats for scraps of food.

Frankly, Natalie was scared. When she put her hands on the table, they stuck there, thanks to a veneer of disgusting glop that covered the table. But the food itself was some of the best I have ever tasted. After a couple of shots of vodka, Natalie began to relax and ignore what was crawling around her feet.

With the help of Gennadi and the Chinese food, Natalie and I grew to accept China quickly. This was unusual for Soviet diplomats, because they mostly tended to walk around pompously, with an air of superiority, and disdained dealing with ordinary people.

So I accepted China, but it cannot be said that China accepted me. Within a few months, I was under almost twenty-four hour surveillance by the Chinese counterintelligence authorities. This wasn't a surprise, because we knew that China devoted 90 percent of its counterintelligence resources to monitoring Soviets. Surveillance was put on all Soviet citizens that left the embassy compound. They had a sort of invisible blockade around the compound, but I soon found its holes.

The day after I arrived, I received my first assignment. I was replacing GRU Lieutenant-Colonel Oleg Mastrukov. Oleg introduced me to his "friend," a Yugoslavian correspondent named Draba. Draba supposedly exchanged information with Oleg. In reality Draba just bought information from the GRU and provided nothing in return.

Draba was what we referred to as a "Paper Agent." Oleg would gather information and then credit it to Draba, which made it appear more valuable to Moscow, and Oleg was congratulated for having developed such a "trusted person" or agent.

> **Our contact preferred "real" Chinese restaurants. After a couple of shots of vodka, Natalie began to relax and ignore what was crawling around her feet.**

It was the first time in my life that I had to deal with this form of cheating, and I didn't like it. The GRU resident, Colonel Vasili Soloviev, already suspected that Draba was a paper agent.

"If you believe he is okay, then we will continue to do business with him," he said. "But if he is a paper agent, don't show it. We will continue to talk to him, but we won't pay attention to him. Since Moscow has already included him in our chain, we don't want to trouble them. Play your games and look around, and some day Draba may come to you and ask for real cooperation. Who knows?"

When Oleg left China a week later, my family moved into his apartment in the embassy. We lived there for a year and a half, until the Chinese government gave us permission to rent an apartment in the city.

I met with Draba a few more times. And I found myself crediting Draba with a few tidbits of information in radio cables back to Moscow. I had to do this so that his validity would not be questioned and call the whole field office into question. But I tried to keep my contact with Draba to a minimum. Beyond the fact that his information was not good, he also had, for a GRU officer like me, undesirable acquaintances. Once when I went to Draba's house, Bill Jones (not his real name), an American correspondent, was also there. When we were introduced, the first thing Jones said was, "So are you from the Red Army or the KGB?"

It's hard to find just the right answer to this question, but I treated it as a joke. "If I were from these groups, I would be very proud of it. And by the way, are you representing the CIA or DIA?"

My "joke" threw him for a small loop. When I reported the conversation to Colonel Soloviev, he told me the GRU believed that Bill Jones was working with or for American intelligence. This also meant that Draba was being targeted by the United States, a helpful thing to know.

Colonel Soloviev was an experienced intelligence officer who was in China as a Soviet military attaché. He knew the "Spy Kitchen" so well that I considered every conversation with him a valuable lesson.

Soloviev left China in September 1980 and was replaced by his deputy, Colonel Evgeni Kalachev, who was assigned as the embassy counselor. His shortcoming was his lack of experience, having previously had only a short assignment in New

York City. He made some poor decisions, the most notable one when he told us to be more active in recruiting foreigners. He said that our dealings with Chinese citizens were being watched carefully, so to show Moscow some progress, we had to target foreigners who were easier to recruit.

"If you don't have any Chinese, show me someone else so that Moscow doesn't question what we are doing."

That was easy for Kalachev to say, but it wasn't easy for me. Members of the foreign press were few in number, and we all knew each other. As for other foreigners, that would mean intruding on the operational areas of other officers who were posing as diplomats or trade representatives. Still, I managed to establish contact with an American I will call Jenny from a major American news service (the last I heard of Jenny was in the early '90s; she was working as a syndicated regional correspondent for southeast Asia). We met a few times at the International Club before I was approached by a KGB officer who told me he had already established contact with Jenny and that I should stay away from her. I told Colonel Kalachev about it and he sent a cable to Moscow. They replied that I should stay away from Jenny, period.

I kept an eye on the situation for a while and concluded that Jenny was another Draba. Paper agents were much too common for my taste.

The same thing happened about a year later, when I tried to recruit Tom, a correspondent with a major midwest newspaper. Again after a meeting with Tom, a KGB colleague came to me and told me to stay away from him. Again Kalachev contacted Moscow, and again I was ordered to stay away. I monitored this situation from a distance and quickly concluded that Tom was probably still another paper agent. (I later ran into Tom in the early 1990s at a White House press conference, where I was accredited as a White House correspondent.) Tom was still reporting for his paper, now as a White House correspondent.

The next time, I won. I met Manolo, a Portuguese correspondent, a few times and reported to Moscow. The GRU approved my recruitment of him as a Trusted Person because he had access to a great deal of information from the Portuguese Embassy, which had excellent relations with China. A little while later, a KGB associate came up to me and asked me to terminate my relationship with Manolo. This time, GRU headquarters told me to continue and the KGB to lay off. It was the informal "Rule of the First Hand" at work—whoever contacts a possible agent first and reports it to Moscow gets to keep the agent.

A practical reason for this, besides possibly drawing too much counterintelligence attention, is that it prevents agents from double-dipping. In a case like Manolo's, it was possible for him to be recruited by the CIA, DIA, GRU, KGB, MI-5, MI-6, and the Mossad. We could at least eliminate conflict between the Soviet agencies.

I had the same success with Charda, a Czechoslovakian news agency correspondent, who was really with the Czechoslovakian intelligence services. But since he was from another Warsaw Pact country, we were not allowed to use him as a full-fledged agent whom we would pay. I could take him only as far as Trusted Person. Moscow told me to be very careful with him, and to try to use his contacts with the

Chinese. Since he was from Czechoslovakia, he was not subject to the travel restrictions that limited us to remaining within twenty-five miles of the center of Tiananmen Square.

In our two years there, Charda and I became close friends, as did our families. We exchanged intelligence information, but we also spent long hours talking about a variety of subjects. His lack of interest in and knowledge of Communist dogmas gave him an open mind, and he opened my mind to some things, such as "the Prague Spring," which was repressed by me and my country in 1968. I don't have any idea where he is now, but I wish him well.

I also recruited Antonio, an Italian correspondent. The Italian Communist Party had close relations with the Chinese Communist Party Central Committee, and, as a result, Antonio had good access to information coming out of the Central Committee. I included Antonio on the GRU chain of Trusted Persons under the code name of "Zag." It became formal when he provided me with an interview he had with Li Xiannian, a senior Chinese leader at that time. Li was using Antonio to inform the Italian government of China's policies and plans in dealing with the USSR.

Obviously, this information was considered "extremely valuable" by the GRU. For me, the most interesting aspect of Antonio was that he was the only foreign correspondent in Beijing who was allowed to live outside the living compounds for foreigners. From time to time, I would visit his small house near Dagulou ("the Tower of a Thousand Jingles") in downtown Beijing.

His neighbors were quite unusual, to put it mildly. Once when I went to visit him, I arrived earlier than expected.

Some Asians who did not look Chinese were playing badminton in his yard. They left immediately on seeing me, but
I remembered their faces. I was shocked several days later
when I saw a picture of Pol Pot, the Cambodian dictator, and
he looked exactly like one of the badminton players. At the
time, Pol Pot was supposedly in hiding, receiving medical
treatment, but we suspected he was hiding in China, which
had officially rejected any involvement in Cambodia's ongo-
ing civil war.

I worked hard on other foreign correspondents, and I
developed close relations with the Kiyodo news agency
bureau chief, Nakajima. He loved Natalie's Russian-style
dumplings, and he was a frequent guest in our home. What
I remember most about him was his Toyota. It was a very
large car in a city of very tiny streets. Once he tried to make
a U-turn on my street and managed to wedge his car
between buildings on opposite sides of the street. We had to
call a tow truck to get him out. To try to recruit him would
have been crazy, since we suspected that he worked for a
Japanese intelligence agency. But I did try to use him as
much as possible.

I also established a good relationship with Carlos, a
Cuban correspondent. He taught me how to make Castro-
style daiquiris out of gin and ice. I also suspected that he was
really with the Cuban military intelligence agency. And I had
friends in the Vietnamese Information Agency (VIA). For
some reason, they were willing to provide me with military-
political information about the Chinese that they were
unwilling to share with any other Soviet correspondents.

Maybe it was because they knew I was in Russian military intelligence and decided I would use the information wisely.

I was friends with many of the other foreign correspondents, but, I admit, all but one of them were operational friendships. The exception was Michael Rank, a Reuters correspondent in Beijing. He was intelligent and extremely loyal to his country, Great Britain. After the second or third meeting, I gave up any hope of using him for intelligence purposes. For a long time, my boss would not accept my arguments that Michael would immediately go to MI-5 or MI-6 if I ever suggested that he do anything to compromise him or his country.

The big thing is that in the war of espionage, nobody really knows who is winning and who is losing.

Of course, I was always on the lookout to recruit Chinese citizens. After all, this was supposed to be the primary job of all GRU, and probably KGB, officers. But it was impossible to meet Chinese people at official press briefings or during visits to government offices. All unauthorized contacts with foreigners was supposed to be reported immediately to the Chinese government. Any violations of that rule were treated not as ordinary crimes, but crimes of treason.

The people who were permitted to have contact with foreigners either worked for, or closely with, the Chinese counterintelligence agencies. At best, you would have a double agent on your hands. But this would lead to problems for the rest of your intelligence career. For that reason, I tried to recruit people only from outside those areas that were closely monitored by the Chinese special services.

If you are caught in any questionable activities by the counterintelligence services, you hope that they just turn you over for deportation. My friend Alex was not so lucky and was hospitalized for a very long time after his handling by the Chinese. It was under the shadow of this that I actually recruited several Chinese nationals.

As a matter of fact, I was the first Soviet operative in at least five years to recruit a Chinese national. There were actually three people I recruited to the point that they were giving me highly classified information. It was in Beijing where I had to use all of my military and espionage training to its fullest, without giving Chinese counterintelligence any clues that I was a GRU officer, and, again, Chinese counter-intelligence officers outnumber foreigners almost one hundred to one.

On a regular basis, I would park between some houses about two miles from the old city in Beijing. Continually on the lookout for surveillance, I would be searching for people moving in the shadows or passing back and forth in front of me. Assuming that all was well, I would stroll through the parks around the town as though I were sightseeing or taking some light exercise.

The parks served as an oasis for the Chinese. These were the only open, peaceful spots for ordinary citizens, who lived in dingy, small, old homes, possibly shared with three generations of relatives. The parks were the only things beautiful in the city. People let down their guards here.

My approach would be to ask a person a question about Chinese culture. The Chinese appreciated my effort to learn, and the fact that I spoke their language so well. I would continue talking to them under the guise that I wanted to practice my Chinese.

If people were willing to meet me several times to practice my Chinese, I would thank them with small gifts and, later, money. The money was very important to them, because they were paid so poorly. This would lead them to give me more information as time went by.

The trick was to get them to know that it was safe to talk and meet with me. They knew they were supposed to report their contact with me. Initially they would be afraid that someone would see us together and they would be arrested. But once they felt that I could ensure their safety, they would open up.

This was how I first handled Zhan. I had almost recruited him to the point of being an agent. He would be the first Chinese recruited by the GRU since Mao Tse-Tung's death five years earlier. My success would have been warmly welcomed by the GRU. He was a student at Beijing University who happened to be the son of the local Army District Division Commander.

Zhan began as my friend. Once I had his confidence, he started bringing me documents, ostensibly to help me with my Chinese in my role as a TASS reporter. I started teaching Zhan how to use dead drops, and recommended that he bring some documents that we could practice with. At this meeting, Zhan shocked me by bringing some very sensitive documents from a Chinese Communist Party Central Committee meeting. This material was highly classified. I did not ask him for any classified materials, and the fact that he was giving me this information was great cause for concern, raising fears that he might be a double agent.

As was standard policy, GRU Resident Kalachev reported this incident to Moscow. The GRU Chief of the Asian Directorate decided that my contact with Zhan was to be terminated immediately. The GRU didn't want to compromise me or other operations. As per my orders, I terminated all contact with Zhan and that was the last we heard of him.

Lu (pronounced Lou) was my second recruit in China. He was an engineer at the Beijing Metallurgy Factory. Metallurgy is an extremely critical science for the military, and intelligence information about it could tell us much about the strengths, weaknesses, and types of Chinese weapons in development. Moreover, this information could help the Soviet Union better compete against the Chinese in arms sales to Third World countries.

Lu was very valuable to the GRU. I met him through the usual method: a chance meeting in a park. I told him that I wanted to improve my knowledge of the Chinese language, and especially in the technical area so that I could add science to my area of reporting for TASS. So he started to bring some technical documents along. For his efforts, I started to give him some small, but slightly valuable, gifts. I started giving Lu cartons of good cigarettes, ball point pens, and other goods that were generally too expensive for Chinese citizens to buy. I told him that I was rewarded by TASS for better articles, and I wanted to pass my rewards on to him. As time went on, I started to give him money and he started to bring classified documents. When I started to give him money, I was very clear that he should not try to show any of his new found wealth. Patriotic—and jealous—the Chinese were notorious for informing on their neighbors if they thought they had too much money.

This type of situation almost resulted in very serious problems for one of my GRU colleagues. Stepan Koldov was supposed to meet with one of his agents and went through the typical routine of making sure that he wasn't being followed. The Zenit post (an electronic, radio, microwave, or other signals' monitoring station within the embassy used for counterintelligence purposes) didn't detect any unusual activity by the Chinese counterintelligence agents, at least until Stepan left his car, and was walking to his meeting about a mile away. Then the Zenit post picked up twenty-four cars and two hundred officers converging on his meeting place. The GRU resident sent out several cars to try to catch him. Luckily he saw one of the Embassy cars go by, which was an automatic sign to call off an operation.

We later learned that Stepan's agent was seen spending too much money, which drew the attention of Chinese counterintelligence. To save himself, the agent agreed to help them catch Stepan. The Chinese were waiting for him with "local citizens," who were there to be outraged by the spy and would beat him to death.

I didn't want that to happen to me, so I was very strict with Lu about how he should behave. I told him not to buy anything expensive, not to go to any new, more expensive restaurants, and not to change any of his habits in general. Despite this, after about six months, he showed up to a meeting wearing some new clothes, which would be too expensive for ordinary Chinese citizens.

I told him that his clothing was unacceptable. He was unrepentant, telling me that this was his only way to get a girlfriend. There were many more men than women in Beijing, and better clothes and expensive gifts were a way to set oneself apart from the competition. I told him the flow of money would end if this kept up, and hoped that he would heed the warning. In fact, during our walk, I noticed we were being followed. It was very amateurish surveillance, but I knew that I had to get Lu out of there. We wandered out of sight of our tails, and I pushed him over a fence into a backyard.

I walked back to the park and struck up a conversation with another Chinese. After a few minutes, I walked away from my reluctant friend and went back to my car. I noticed that my tail went after the poor Chinese man I'd left behind in the park. I felt sorry for him.

Again, I had *almost* recruited him to be a full agent. I never saw Lu again, but my successor might have. After I returned to Moscow, I would occasionally ask about him and was told that it was none of my business. I interpreted that as a good sign.

I met Zhao, who I actually did recruit to the status of agent, in Violet Bamboo Park on a sunny spring day. I noticed old men in the park, holding bird cages. I asked Zhao why? He told me a Chinese tradition: "If you bring out your bird in the spring and summer, in a place where they can hear all the sounds of nature, they will have songs in their hearts throughout the rest of the year."

I told him how I was a reporter trying to improve my language. He told me he worked at the Central Railway Station for Beijing. As time went on, he agreed to meet with me later.

I soon learned that his father had been punished by the communists for being an educated man, and that his aunt had been killed in a random street crime. His uncle had just disappeared one day. Zhao feared—and he was not kidding—that his uncle had been chopped up for a South Chinese delicacy known as three-meat dumpling. One of the meats during the Chinese cultural revolution was sometimes… people.

Zhao himself was very poor and could not adequately support himself and his family. As he started to bring me technical information "to help me learn Chinese," I gave him some small presents as a token of my appreciation; later I gave him money, telling him that it was passed on from TASS.

Zhao's information was extremely valuable. The Beijing Central Railway Station was the choke point for all rail transportation in the country. Zhao had access to all train manifests and knew what was being transported to and through Beijing, including troop movements.

But getting Zhao's information was not easy. Typically, I started out in the early afternoon and would wander around Beijing trying to make sure that I was not being followed. After that I would hide my car and work my way to a railroad bridge. Sometimes, if I was under heavy surveillance, I would ride in the trunk of another GRU operative's car. When it was safe, he would let me out in an alley. In any event, I typically tried to meet agents at night, in the dark, so that my European looks would not attract attention.

The only way I could reach the old part of Beijing was to cross over a river and a canal. All bridges, however, were considered strategic in China, and were guarded by soldiers. The railroad bridge was perfect for my purposes. As the train approached the bridge, it would slow down for boarding soldiers. This made it easy for me to jump between the wheels of the train, and grab onto an axle or support. I would then ride below the train as it went by the guards.

I was good at this. I'd been trained for it. As part of my Deep Reconnaissance training, I was required to jump in between the wheels of a train traveling at full speed, because I was expected to use the enemy's transportation system as my own. When we were past the guards, I would let go and wait for the rest of the train to roll over me. From there I would roll into the bushes. Then I made it through the dark streets of the Old City—streets with names like Dragon's Cave Road. On one strange night, after I dodged through bushes, alleys, and backyards, and past fornicating couples seeking to escape the eyes of the authorities, I came to a canal I had to cross. I did this by walking along a water pipe that was about six inches wide, and suspended about fifteen feet above the water. The canal was filled with snakes and rats, both dead and alive. Still, I made it to the other side, and jumped into the bushes on the bank of the canal.

I was quickly surrounded by four street criminals who were divvying up their night's booty. After a bit of yelling, I could tell they were going to attack me. The leader pulled out a knife, as did one of his friends. The other two thieves pulled nunchakus (a martial arts weapon that has two sticks, about eighteen inches long, connected by a metal chain).

I was in several jams. Obviously, I could have been killed, but I wasn't afraid of that. If these criminals figured out that I was a foreigner, they could report me to the Chinese authorities. Then the Chinese would be watching my way over the canal for the rest of my tour. If I killed any of the criminals, there would be an investigation and the police would watch this area in the future. Still I had to hurt the criminals enough so that they couldn't follow me.

I deflected the first knife attack and hit the assailant in the solar plexus. I then got another two in the groin, and gave the last one an elbow to his head. They were not getting up anytime soon, and I made my way to the meeting place with Zhao. My last obstacle was a park. At night, this park was locked, with guard dogs patrolling it. However from the time I arrived in Beijing, I made it a point to make these dogs my friends. I would always bring food with me on my late night travels. I would feed the dogs and let them sniff me to the point where they would know me and let me pass without attacking. This night I also had some food with me, and my friends let me pass to the other side.

Then I saw Zhao, and we greeted each other with a friendly, "Nin Hao," or "Hey Guy" in Chinese. Of course, I never told him the extremes that I went through to get to him. On this night, he told me how his girlfriend was also willing to pass information to me. This was something that I did not want to hear. The fact that his girlfriend knew that he was giving me information was not good, but the information she did have was valuable and Zhao was outliving his usefulness to the GRU.

Zhao's girlfriend, Jiang, worked in a trade ministry as a secretary. As Zhao explained to me, the secretaries did all the work for their bosses. The bosses just signed whatever the secretaries asked them to. It turned out that Jiang's office was responsible for negotiating arms sales to African countries, which was very useful information to help us undercut their deals with Soviet competition. I made sure that Zhao helped train Jiang in acquiring information so as not to cause suspicion.

I was beginning to worry about when the GRU would ask me to terminate my relationship with Zhao. If he was ever caught by the Chinese, he would be lucky if he was killed quickly. Before my last meeting with Zhao, he broke up with Jiang and had a new girlfriend, who had even more access than Jiang did. But our relationship ended before I judged her usefulness. During one meeting, I detected that we were being followed. I quickly changed directions so that we had one or two more minutes together. This gave me enough time to give Zhao some money and remind him of the location and time of our next meeting. I then walked him over to the dark side of the street and told him to go in a different direction. I walked up to another person who was dressed like him. I asked him where the nearest bus stop was. As before, the surveillance followed the Good Samaritan instead of me. I was then ordered to stop contacting Zhao, though I was happy to learn that counterintelligence never found him.

Several months later, Zhao used fake documents (which I provided) to sneak out of China to Singapore. He made his way from Singapore to Australia to Canada, and then to New York. In New York, he was found by the uncle he thought had been made into dumplings. His uncle was actually involved with Chinese gangs and brought Zhao into the business.

I found this out almost a decade later, when I was stationed in Washington. I was on a trip to New York, and Zhao found me. Apparently his gang kept better surveillance on TASS correspondents than the FBI did. He also told me that he had a relative working for Northrup Corporation who was involved in creating Stealth technology. For $1 million, he was willing to get me almost anything I wanted on Stealth fighters and bombers. I did not accept his offer—I knew the GRU already had the information it needed on Stealth technology.

My tour in China pushed my skills to their limits. Never have I been so outnumbered by the enemy as I was in China, and never was my life at greater continuous risk. But the big thing is that in the war of espionage, nobody really knows who is winning and who is losing.

Chapter 11

ASSIGNMENT: AMERICA

WHEN I RETURNED TO MOSCOW in December 1983, I was ordered to see Lieutenant General Vladimir Molchanov, the Second GRU Directorate (Asia) chief. We called him "Funny Boy" because nobody had ever seen him smile. I stood in front of him as he sat there expressionless for several minutes.

"You guys in Beijing, are you still getting rid of your tails?" was how he broke the silence.

As I started to answer, he interrupted me in midsentence to tell his aide, navy Commander Romyntsev, "Send a cable to Beijing and tell them to stop getting rid of their tails." Then to me, he said: "Your tour in Beijing was extremely successful. You are free." His few words were plentiful reward for my work in Beijing, until I learned that Molchanov was forced to retire two years later for taking bribes. But at the time, I was full of respect for the man that was leading our intelligence efforts against China and other Asian countries.

After I left Molchanov, I asked Commander Gennadi Romyntsev, "Why all the ruckus about losing our tails?" He said that soon after my departure, military officers in uniform made a ritual of losing their tails every day, and in response, the Chinese stepped up their counterintelligence efforts to the point where we could do nothing because the surveillance was too tight.

Mikhail Gorbachev's anti-alcohol campaign destroyed the economy and pumped up the black market. This expanded the "shadow economy" that led to the growth and power of organized crime.

I was now a lieutenant colonel, and for my next assignment I was appointed to the GRU Operational Group in TASS of the First GRU Subdirectorate—or "the furniture store."

For the next three years, I spent up to six hours a day reading about China and other assigned countries and writing stories about them. I also ran all over town trying to develop contacts with foreigners and develop information I could feed to the Information Directorates of the GRU. In addition, I was asked to teach journalism to new GRU officers.

In my second year at TASS, I was promoted to senior operations officer. The next year, I was promoted to deputy commander of the GRU Operational Group in TASS; and at the beginning of 1988, to group commander/GRU resident in TASS. All GRU officers at TASS now reported to me. I was also promoted to the rank of full colonel.

I was very happy with my life and career. I now had more time to enjoy sports, movies, plays, libraries, and sightseeing.

My family was well off, by Soviet standards. Soon after our return from China, we received a new apartment in a prestigious Moscow neighborhood, Krilatskoe, where Yeltsin and his closest associates are living now. And with the money we had saved, we were able to buy a small car.

But things were not going well in the Soviet Union. The war in Afghanistan was killing tens of thousands of young soldiers, including many of my friends. I volunteered several times, but I was told that I was much more valuable to the Soviet Union in Moscow. To an infantry soldier like myself, this hurt.

I prepared to face my country's principal enemy. I attended special training in American tactics and how to counter them.

The Soviet economy was also crumbling. Stores were empty of almost everything. Mikhail Gorbachev's anti-alcohol campaign helped to destroy the economy and pump up the black market for alcohol. This helped expand the "shadow economy" that led to the growth and power of organized crime.

It was then that I was told to prepare myself for a new assignment—to the United States. This was a major change. I was already assigned to go to Laos, and was looking forward to it. There is only one TASS correspondent assigned to that country, and that meant that I would be relatively independent. More important, Laos was a friendly country with little surveillance and had plenty of foreigners for me to shop among. A good salary, little oversight, little surveillance, plenty of foreigners—what could be better for an experienced intelligence officer?

My daughter was also graduating from high school and wanted to attend Moscow University. But I was needed immediately in the United States and couldn't stay in Moscow to help her get into a university—a difficult achievement in the Soviet Union because there were ten applicants for every position.

When I told my commanders why I wanted to go to Laos instead of the United States, the answer from all of them was the same, "Shut up, and go."

As usual, I was a good soldier and responded with a loud, "Yes, sir!" So, now I prepared to face my country's principal adversary. I attended special training in American tactics and how to counter them, and I worked at the American desk at TASS for the appropriate cover training.

In August 1988, Natalie and I left Moscow with mixed feelings. When we went to China, we were prepared for everything and felt comfortable with it. This time we were not so certain. Maybe we knew that we would not be coming back.

Chapter 12

MY "ARRIVAL"

MY FIRST GRU ASSIGNMENT in a capitalist country, Singapore, helped to solidify my belief that capitalism was inherently evil. I saw billionaires living in mansions, and just down the street, children living in cardboard boxes. I was expecting to see the same thing when I was transferred to America. My attitude changed as my flight approached Dulles airport, just outside Washington, DC. I looked out the window and noticed the ground was shimmering. I couldn't figure why and asked Natalie. She didn't know.

"They're swimming pools," the Russian sitting next to her said with a smile.

I couldn't believe it. There were hundreds of them down there in Virginia. This couldn't be. After all if there were this many pools, there had to be a huge middle class, and I knew that that was impossible. If the American middle class was that large, then everything I had been told about the evils of capitalism was a lie, and I soon came to conclude that it was.

On my arrival in Washington in August 1988, I was at a distinct disadvantage. Alexander, my predecessor, had worked extremely hard as an intelligence agent, but he was not a good journalist, which was bad for his cover as a TASS correspondent.

The situation was so bad that the "clean" correspondents were giving him all of the odd jobs that they didn't want to do. Alexander would also frequently drive while drunk, and on one occasion was stopped by the police. So the GRU chief returned Alexander to Moscow.

Mid-level officers in the Third Directorate of the GRU—who didn't want to take responsibility for allowing an alcoholic to rise through the ranks—described the drunk driving incident as an FBI "provocation." Today Alexander is officially retired from the GRU and is back in the states as a correspondent with ITAR-TASS in New York City.

> **It is common knowledge among GRU and SVR radio officers that the FBI has equipped the major entrances and exits of the Washington, DC, beltway with receivers to pick up secret transmitters placed on the cars of foreign intelligence operatives.**

For my first few weeks in Washington, I lived with Natalie in the compound at the Soviet Embassy on Mount Alto.

On our first weekend, Natalie and I decided to explore the local area. It was a beautiful August Sunday morning and the streets were not too crowded. We were being typical tourists, just looking around, window-shopping as we walked along and trying to find the sites that we had read about in the tourist guidebooks. I soon realized that we were under surveillance. I heard some noise, and turned to see a beautiful woman jogging. She looked almost like a *Sports Illustrated* model. It was very difficult not to remember her. In fact, I had seen her an hour before. I looked around and found she wasn't alone. I must thank the FBI for making a great first impression.

Ironically, a couple of years later, I was almost robbed on Pennsylvania Avenue right across the street from FBI headquarters. There never seems to be a cop around when you need one. Two robbers came up to me and asked me for $20. I told them that I didn't have that much money. They heard my accent and asked where I was from. When I told them the Soviet Union, they said that they should be helping me instead of robbing me. They started laughing and just walked away. They only had a knife, and by looking at their eyes, I knew they were harmless. If forced to fight, I would have.

I have a great deal of respect for the FBI and other U.S. counterintelligence officers. The other Soviet intelligence officers and I never knew exactly which group our tails were from. The FBI has the largest counterintelligence operation, but we could also be followed by the CIA or by intelligence officers from the Army, Navy, Marines, or especially the Air Force. Since the Manhattan Project, the Air Force has been very active in counterintelligence.

The U.S. counterintelligence services are superlative, and the FBI's standards are extremely high. Many of their agents have advanced degrees and must have at least two years of professional experience before applying to the service. Their main training facility is in Quantico, Virginia, and they have offices all over the United States and in major cities around the world. They also have some of the most advanced surveillance technology anywhere, including specially designed cars, helicopters, airplanes, and even satellites.

In high espionage areas, the FBI has established what amounts to surveillance shields. For example, it is common knowledge among GRU and SVR radio officers that the FBI has equipped the major entrances and exits of the Washington, DC, beltway with receivers to pick up secret transmitters placed on the cars of foreign intelligence operatives. It was almost impossible to avoid using the beltway, but my compatriots and I were forced to do so when engaged in covert action.

The Washington area is swarming with spies from nearly every country in the world, and the one big problem for American counterintelligence is that they are woefully underfunded, given the scope of their problem. GRU officers knew this and took advantage of it whenever possible. The overload of work on American counterintelligence was a critical part of our planning.

We used our knowledge of the FBI's modus operandi to help plan our primary mission. If someone was under surveillance for a day, we knew that the surveillance would last for at least a week. If it continued into a second week, it would go on for at least a month. When we knew we were under surveillance, we would avoid anything suspicious and take the time to do our "clean" job. When this time was up, we would do our real job.

These rules were good for normal activity, but not for special events, such as meetings with agents or dead drops that were scheduled months or years in advance. During these special events, we took further advantage of FBI predictability. There were four permanent FBI monitoring posts with about two dozen cars assigned for surveillance around the Soviet Embassy. When one officer had to go to a meeting and was probably being watched, we would summon at least twenty-four operatives, who we knew were considered registered spies by the FBI, to the embassy. They would leave the embassy at around the same time, taking with them all the tails. The FBI would call for reinforcements, but in the interval, an officer could generally leave without being followed.

> I was amazed—and Moscow was very appreciative—at how many times I found very sensitive information in American newspapers. Americans care more about scooping their competition than about national security, which made my job easier.

Another example of surveillance that I experienced on a regular basis was at the National Press Building. In the TASS offices, there was a small lobby with a table and a couple of chairs that were used by the few visitors we had. I am certain that this area was bugged by the FBI, and perhaps under photo surveillance, because when a light bulb burned out, a special crew would come in and change it immediately. This crew wouldn't change any other burnt out bulb, even if we asked them to.

I used this situation to enhance my cover. Whenever I was busy with my "clean" duties, I would try to write my stories and columns in the lobby to impress the FBI with my innocence. But my KGB counterparts, I found, used the lobby as a working area to write their Top Secret reports so that they wouldn't be seen by the other TASS reporters. I tried to warn them, but in true KGB fashion, they refused to admit that what they were doing was stupid, and continued the practice. Probably as a result of this insanity, they were under constant FBI surveillance, while I seemed to get minimal attention.

From time to time, however, I created my own problems. The first one was soon after my arrival. Usually for the first six months at a new station, a GRU officer lies low. But I found that the GRU station chiefs were not going to enforce these limitations on me. So four days after my arrival, I made my first official visit to the Soviet Embassy under cover of registering with the embassy Communist Party organization. I went to a special area with a steel door, entered a special code given to me in Moscow, and I was in the most restricted area of the Soviet Embassy, the GRU field office. In a few minutes, I found some old friends and met new colleagues, and they showed me the way to the office of the GRU Resident, Captain German Fotigarov, whom I had never met.

When I introduced myself, Captain Fotigarov and I followed standard GRU procedures, not mentioning our names or ranks. After a few minutes, Fotigarov surprised me with two unusual statements.

"Don't even think about staying in the GRU apartment in the embassy compound for more than one week," he told me. "You have a right to rent an apartment in the city. Do so!"

"Excuse me, sir," I replied, "but TASS and the State Department are negotiating this, and I don't have any idea when it will be resolved."

"That is your problem," he said abruptly, and changed the subject.

A few minutes later he surprised me again: "Do you know about the American document, the *Congressional Presentation for the National Security Assistance in 1988?*"

"Nyet."

Captain Fotigarov showed me a secret cable sent from GRU headquarters in Moscow, ordering him to find the document and send it to Moscow via "Commander's Mail"—a secret shipping route between GRU residents and GRU headquarters. The cable gave no information about which institution had written or published the document, or anything else besides the title.

"Your cover is most suitable for this job, so do it," he ordered. "And don't forget about moving out of the embassy compound by the end of the week. Goodbye!"

I left the embassy and reached a large window on H Street. I decided to stop at the window to see if I was being followed. I noticed that the window looked into the Government Printing Office bookstore, and after taking a closer look, I saw right inside the window a book entitled, *Congressional Presentation for the National Security Assistance in 1988.*

"Bingo," was the only thing that went through my mind.

I bought the book and left, my first assignment satisfied within an hour. It took a couple of days to move out of the embassy compound and into my new place at The Hamlet in Alexandria. At the end of my first full week, I took the book to Captain Fotigarov feeling as if I had just won my first battle, but I quickly learned that it was too early to blow the trumpets.

As Captain Fotigarov thumbed through the book, I realized that he had never seen this document before and didn't know the *Congressional Presentation* was published every year. It had some incredibly valuable information about U.S. foreign and military aid—valuable information that the Americans, typically, were willing to give away in public documents.

"This book is fine, but where were you yesterday?" Fotigarov demanded.

"At the Nuclear Regulatory Commission, sir."

"What did you do there?"

"I was covering a press conference at the request of TASS, and I had an interview with the commission director, who had just returned from Moscow and wanted to speak about the future of nuclear cooperation between our two countries," I replied.

"Who gave you permission to go there?" he demanded.

"Sir," I said, starting to feel like shit, "it was a fast request from Moscow, and the TASS bureau chief asked me to put everything else on hold and go immediately. What did I do wrong?"

"You never, remember, *never* go anywhere that is registered in our Yellow Book without my permission," he warned. "Have you seen it?"

I explained that since my arrival in Moscow, I had spent only an hour in the field office and wasn't familiar with the local procedures. No one in Moscow had told me anything about a Yellow Book.

"I'll forget about it, but only once," Fotigarov replied.

He then produced the mysterious book, which was simply a list of hundreds of American agencies and businesses, many highlighted in yellow, such as the Nuclear Regulatory Commission, the National Security Agency, NASA, Boeing, Martin Marietta, GE, the Congressional Printing Office, and others.

"Yellow marks mean that these agencies and companies are already covered by our people, and we have enough information about them," he explained. "Yesterday, your trip to the NRC could have increased the FBI's attention on it and you. We don't need that type of attention."

"But, sir, my operational tasking describes the House Armed Forces Committee as an 'object for penetration by agents,' but it's in yellow. What does this mean?"

"It means that you need to forget all about it. Later, I will provide you with a new place for penetration. Sometimes Moscow doesn't really know what's going on here," Fotigarov said. I didn't need to ask how he knew of my visit to the NRC. The Zenit post at the GRU field office registers the movements of any operative who is a target of unusual surveillance. Since I was on official TASS business, I didn't care if I was being followed by the FBI. In fact, I would have welcomed their watching me perform my official duties. But the Zenit post was invaluable to those GRU operatives who were not sure if they were being followed.

As it turned out, during my first two years in Washington I was assigned no official tasking. I had to find and recruit agents wherever I could, other than people associated with organizations highlighted in the Yellow Book.

I was successful because in the Washington area, it is almost impossible not to find people with classified access. You could meet them at just about any official function, or restaurant for that matter. I met one of my most valuable agents during my first winter in Washington at a press conference at the National Resources Defense Council. (In fear of endangering his life, all I can reveal about Jim is that he worked for a think tank.) I quickly learned that he was having problems making ends meet—he needed money.

This was a classical recruitment task and took months to develop—not the quick job the movies like to paint. I began to meet Jim on a regular basis, at first merely to get his opinions for use in my TASS columns. After a while, I began to pay him for some of his information and he grew to rely on the money. As time went on, the questions became more sensitive and the payments grew larger. Soon he was giving me whatever he could.

Within six months, I had several major "friendships" with foreign and American journalists, people who work for U.S. government agencies, and people in private organizations.

In the spring of 1989, there was a major shakeup at the GRU field office in Washington. Captain Fotigarov was demoted to deputy chief, and Major General Grigoriy Yakovlev was brought in as the new GRU resident. Because of his vast experience in intelligence and his reputation for not putting up with incompetence, most of the GRU officers were scared of him. I was not too worried because I was confident about the quality of my work and didn't believe I had anything to be afraid of. At the time, I was assigned to a subgroup consisting of four people who were responsible for military-political information. (Other subgroups covered economic, scientific, arms control, and other such issues.)

We had to write daily cables summarizing important issues or events, focusing on anything dealing with U.S. intentions toward the Soviet Union and its allies.

I spent the bulk of my time writing these cables. I was amazed—and Moscow was very appreciative—at how many times I found very sensitive information in American newspapers. In my view, Americans tend to care more about scooping their competition than about national security, which made my job easier.

I also had to develop a personal schedule that would satisfy my cover assignment as a reporter. That took only four to five hours a day. I was proud to learn, after I defected, that the FBI was never certain whether I was actually a spy because they thought I worked better and harder than reporters they knew to be "clean."

I spent another four to five hours a day performing my GRU tasks. This included establishing new contacts, widening my circle of acquaintances, and acquiring information for the Soviet government. Three more hours were spent in the GRU field office, talking to my boss and other intelligence officers, sharing information, and writing cables.

My first meeting with General Yakovlev was actually pleasant. I went into his office to have him sign, as was required, my daily cable to Moscow. I handed him the paper. He read it, signed it, and gave it to the clerk to be encoded and sent. We then spent an hour talking about things in general. Before I left, he said that my work was "not very bad," which was an encouraging sign.

A few weeks later he removed me from my operational group and made me his personal subordinate, responsible for meeting emergency requests from GRU headquarters. My agents and contacts in Washington were recognized as highly valuable sources for military-political information.

Under the leadership of General Yakovlev, I was able to spend much more time traveling around the city, meeting and developing contacts, and obtaining information. By August 1989, my information was reaching the highest levels of the Soviet military-political establishment, and to Gorbachev himself. As a spy, I had definitely "arrived."

This level of visibility was a sign of my success, but, as is the case with most people, I had other problems. My work schedule was taking its toll on my family, and my daughter's marriage—she had opted to marry rather than attend a university—was beginning to fall apart. Overall, though, it was a good first year.

Chapter 13

WORLD WAR III

I WAS EXHAUSTED from searching the entire Washington, DC, area for a new dead drop site. This is one of the hardest tasks for many spies, because most of the good sites have already been "discovered" by other operatives. There is also competition because the different operatives vie to report the newly discovered site to Moscow as quickly as possible. The FBI presents another problem, because they occasionally discover the sites. Eventually, I found a spot in the Great Falls area of Maryland.

Although I was tired, I was delighted with my excellent site. When I got home, I looked forward to a warm welcome and a good dinner. But that was not to be. Natalie right away insisted that I take the garbage down to its spot in the basement.

"I'll do it after dinner," I said, disgruntled. After a day of evading the FBI and watching for tails at every turn, I was in no mood to worry about the damned garbage.

"Do it now. I'll help you with it," Natalie said—and then winked.

She knew that our apartment was being bugged by the FBI. We knew where the bugs were, but we left them alone. Removing them would only have brought suspicion on us—and new bugs.

Downstairs, Natalie handed me a piece of paper with the words, "You need to be at your place in the embassy at 10:00 AM tomorrow. Good Luck! Alex."

> We knew that our apartment was being bugged by the FBI. Removing them would only have brought suspicion on us—and new bugs.

KGB Major Alex Berodzkov was officially a TASS correspondent in Washington. (As of this writing, he is officially retired from the KGB and assigned to the TASS bureau in New York City.)

I knew it was an "emergency call," because the station chief would not normally use a KGB officer to contact a GRU officer. It was a violation of protocol. The possible emergency could be anything from our going to war to my being called upon to do a "dirty job."

Early the next morning I went to the National Press Building to do some research—and "spin" my counterintelligence shadows. Within the earshot of the bugs, I mentioned to a colleague that I had to go to the embassy to meet with the cultural attaché, Comrade Alexander Potemkin, to research a story on development of cultural relations between the United States and the USSR. My TASS Bureau Chief had been hassling me to write about this for a while. Now it was the perfect cover.

At 9:55, I reported to my chief, Major General Yakovlev.

"Take a seat," said General Yakovlev, in a bad mood.

I was the only person who didn't fear him.

"These f— bosses in Moscow believe we have influence over White House and presidential decisions," said Yakovlev as he handed me a paper marked "Top Secret." "Look at it," he demanded.

U.S. Marine Lieutenant Colonel Higgins had recently been executed by Islamic terrorists. In response the U.S. Sixth Fleet's battle group was sent to the Mediterranean. In a few days it would reach Lebanon. Soviet naval intelligence didn't have access to the fleet commander's orders. So GRU headquarters ordered us to (1) Discover America's plans; (2) If a military strike was in the works, report what types of weapons would be used; and (3) Discover what the administration wanted to achieve. Everything was to be reported to Moscow by the end of the day.

According to the top secret message, the Politburo was considering a military response to any blow against the Soviet Union's Arab allies.

"I think the American commanders don't know what they are supposed to do, and George Bush doesn't either," Yakovlev said. "But you have about seven hours to find real answers. I will wait for you here. Good luck."

At 11:30 that morning, I was down in a special section of the National Press Building. Here foreign correspondents met with about a dozen U.S. officials who served as formal contacts between us and U.S. government agencies. But the officials pulled "double duty." For example, we believed that John, who was our contact with the Department of State, was actually with the CIA. Kathy, who was our congressional contact, was really with the FBI. My official contact, and friend, was Thomas, an air force colonel representing the Department of Defense. By noon, I was listening to Thomas's view of what the Joint Chiefs of Staff would tell President Bush: "Don't hit Lebanon, but scare them with the threat that we might." I officially listed him as a Trusted Person, and considered his information reliable, but I had to confirm it with other sources.

At 1:00 PM, I was two floors down in my friend David's office. He was a well-respected correspondent with a U.S. military magazine. I had listed him as a possible Trusted Person, though he didn't know it. He had close contacts with the U.S. military-political establishment and always seemed able to get his hands on information. While I never gave him money for information, I would pay him in kind. If I had information he wanted—or could get it from Moscow—and it was not too sensitive, I would give it to him.

"What's going on with the U.S. battle group in the Mediterranean?" I asked him in the middle of a dozen questions.

"You know," he said openly, "my editors have already asked me this question. I told them that according to my sources, it would be some kind of demonstration of power, because it's a difficult time in the Mideast. Any violence in the area would damage our interests much more than any benefit we could derive from a direct strike against terrorists. Besides, if we couldn't find the terrorists holding Higgins, how are we to find the terrorist hiding places while avoiding killing innocent civilians?"

Given the stakes, I didn't stop with two sources. At about 2:40 PM, I used a pay phone near the Riggs Bank on Pennsylvania Avenue, almost across the street from the White House, to call my friend at the think tank. He knew that I needed to meet with him immediately by a few prearranged code words that I threw into the call. Twenty minutes later, Jim met me at Starbuck's Coffee Shop on K Street.

Jim was writing a book on *glasnost* and *perestroika*, and appreciated the connections we'd given him at Leningrad State University, along with money for his research. While nobody ever told Jim that he owed the Soviet government anything, he appeared to "understand" this.

Jim had access to much sensitive information. He had many friends on the National Security Council and in the administration. With Jim, I never had to hide my intentions. He was a fully recruited agent. Within fifteen minutes, I had all that I wanted. Apparently the National Security Council was going to meet that night to develop a recommendation for the president on the Lebanese situation. The general advice to President Bush was, "Stay away from any direct involvement."

With three separate and reliable sources providing the same information, I was ready to return to General Yakovlev.

When I reported to his office at 5:00 PM, he was not alone. The naval attaché, Captain Ilushenko, and the Signals Intelligence post chief were also awaiting my answer. But only Yakovlev was allowed to ask me any questions.

It took me only a minute to tell him that the current American deployment was only a show of power.

"Ilushenko had the same information from his sources at the Office of the Chief of Naval Operations," said Yakovlev. "We know from him that the commander of the battle group hasn't received any orders from Washington. Wait while I finish the cable for Moscow. I need the code names of the sources you spoke to. I think that you will all agree with my recommendation not to heat up the problem and reserve pressuring the United States for a more strategic time. Thanks to all of you."

At 6:30 PM my TASS bureau chief was delighted to see me at my desk writing a story on cultural relations between the United States and the USSR. He was so happy that he invited me into his office and secretly gave me a couple of tickets to the Soviet circus that was soon to appear at George Mason University. Little did he know I was concerned only about covering my tracks with the FBI.

"Here's everything you'll need to write a small story about the performance," he said. "You know, those reporters out there are driving me crazy asking for these tickets. But I kept them specifically for you, because I know that you won't cheat on me."

I hate the circus, but I realized that these tickets were to be my only reward for a job well done on two separate fronts. That's how it works in the real spy world. You avert World War III, and what do you get? Circus tickets.

Chapter 14

MY SPIES

I LEFT MY TASS OFFICE at the National Press Building early. It was a sunny summer morning in 1990. I spent the day driving to sites that helped with my official cover. As dusk set in, I watched closely for surveillance. When I was sure that I was not being followed, I drove my Mercury Sable to a small parking lot on Little River Turnpike just outside the beltway. I put up the hood of my car, as if I were having engine problems, and sat three feet from a dirty pay phone waiting for it to ring.

If the telephone rang three times, and then three times more a few minutes later, I was being followed. The Zenit had been listening to FBI radio frequencies throughout the day to ascertain whether any agents might be tailing me. I sat listening to the birds and making sure nobody else used the phone.

The telephone was quiet. I decided it was safe to go to the drop site. I drove to a secluded road in northern Virginia, stopped, and picked up a Coca Cola can on the side of the road. It was like one of those cans with a screw lid that people buy in specialty stores to stash their jewelry and thwart burglars, except this one was designed by the GRU to destroy its contents should it be opened by someone other than the GRU. It was also excellent for storing film canisters.

I picked up the can and took it back with me to the embassy. I had to be very careful with the can, because cans like this were usually rigged to explode or to spill acid if someone tried to open them. I took the can to the GRU specialists to open.

If the telephone rang three times, and then three times more a few minutes later, I was being followed.

The film, which had come from Jim (code name Don), was the transcript of a closed hearing of the Senate Intelligence Committee discussing U.S. strategy on the disintegration of the Soviet Union. The discussion included sensitive details about agents and operations against the Soviet Union. It was valuable information, and Jim was handsomely rewarded.

Another of my valuable Trusted Persons was John (code name Rob), the U.S. air force lieutenant colonel assigned as the Department of Defense liaison to foreign reporters.

During Operations Desert Shield and Storm, John gave me four boxes of documents that detailed the technical characteristics of every weapons system employed in the Persian Gulf. There was one box each for the Army, Navy, Air Force, and Marines.

John also invited me to a special show for NATO officials and reporters at Andrews Air Force Base. The show was to demonstrate the next generation of high-tech weapons, specifically B-2 bombers, Stealth fighters, and advanced cruise missiles. The show took place in a closed hangar, protected by armed security police and dogs, and accessible only by a special bus. I was able to walk around the hangar and take many, many pictures with both my TASS camera and a specially outfitted GRU camera. My main target for the GRU camera was the tail section of the B-2 bomber. (Previously, I had attended an open-air show at Andrews Air Force Base. The GRU had provided me with special transparent gloves that collected material from whatever they came in contact with. I was told to touch an F-117 fighter, if at all possible. When some small children jumped over a fence, distracting everyone including the guards, I was able to touch an F-117. The gloves collected valuable samples of Stealth composites.)

I brought the GRU camera back to the embassy, when it was sent to Moscow via a fast and secure Aeroflot plane. I then took the film from the TASS camera to a supermarket to have it developed. When I got the pictures back several days later, they were placed in neat photo albums, one album per roll. I packaged some of these albums and sent them to the Aeroflot office for shipment to TASS headquarters in Moscow. From there, TASS might place them in a few magazines or newspapers.

I also decided to take a few albums to the embassy to show the other GRU officers. When I showed them to General Yakolev, he yelled, "I thought you were supposed to send all your pictures to the GRU!" I told him that I had sent the camera back to Moscow as instructed. He then took out a secret cable from GRU headquarters requesting that if I had any more pictures, I should send them to GRU as well.

Yakolev started shouting that I had forgotten whom I was really working for—the GRU—that I was stupid, and on and on. He had me go to the Aeroflot office on K and 16th Streets and get the package before the next flight took off. But this was a Saturday, and the Aeroflot office was closed. I went back and reported this to Yakolev. He ordered me to go back and wait. So I went, and waited, as ordered.

It was a hot windy day, and garbage was flying all over the place as I sat there on the street with the homeless and crazy people. I began to notice that I was under surveillance. At least I knew that I wouldn't have to worry about being mugged, with all those FBI agents around. After three hours of waiting and feeling stupid, I saw a GRU car drive by. Without stopping they gave me a signal that told me to go back to the embassy.

When I got there, I was told that the deputy ambassador had found the Aeroflot representative. Aeroflot would not send out any packages until I got the pictures back.

John also got me invited to a chemical destruction facility on Johnston Island, near Hawaii, which also happened to be the location of a strategic American nuclear test facility. This was the first time that a Soviet intelligence officer was able to go there. Someone at the State Department might have actually realized the strategic importance of the site, because they weren't as helpful as they usually were. When I notified the

State Department where I was going, they seemed surprised. They even called back several times to confirm that I had an invitation from the Department of Defense to go to a highly sensitive facility.

When I arrived in Hawaii, I had an immediate assignment. I was to collect all possible information about downtown Honolulu, especially the area around Fort DeRussy, that would be useful for future illegal operational and support missions. After checking into my hotel, I changed my clothes and grabbed my cameras. I bought a local map at the hotel gift shop and tried to take advantage of a few more hours of daylight. I started taking pictures of Beachwalk Street, Kalakava Avenue, Ala Moana Boulevard, and other convenient streets.

The best spy will be everyone's best friend, not a shadowy figure in the corner.

Trying to give the FBI the impression that I was just overwhelmed by the beauty of the local area, I also took pictures of the local stores, restaurants, cafeterias, and so on. I tried to take "artsy" types of pictures that included garbage cans, street lights, saleswomen, and newspaper machines. I was so unconcerned about the local FBI, because of my successful cover, that I accidentally took a picture of the FBI agents who were following me, while I was on Kalakava Avenue. Of course, this was also their mistake.

After that accident I had continued "Demonstration Surveillance." This is where you have people ten feet in front and in back of you at all times. I had them at beaches, shops, restrooms, elevators, and everywhere along the way. The only time they left my side was when I passed onto military bases.

When I was there, the U.S. Army counterintelligence officers had jurisdiction.

The next day, while it was still dark, I found myself at Fort DeRussy in the company of about two dozen other foreign correspondents. All of them were from "friendly" countries. We sat through several hours of safety training, and were taught and tested on how to use gas masks. I had to make them believe that this was my first time using a mask and that I was clueless on American military terminology, when in fact I had been practicing putting gas masks on since I was eleven years old. Still, I had to make myself look stupid or I would give myself away. I wasn't sure how successful I had been until later that day. In the men's room I overheard one of the instructors say: "All these guys look like they're spies, except that crazy Russian guy from TASS. He really doesn't have any idea about military stuff, and almost suffocated himself during the gas mask tests."

At 4:00 AM the next morning, the FBI followed me through the totally deserted streets of Honolulu to Fort DeRussy. There, a U.S. Army bus took all of the correspondents to Hickam Air Force Base at Pearl Harbor. An hour later, we were aboard a C-141 headed for Johnston Island. It took about two hours for us to reach the island specifically located at 16 degrees 45 minutes North by 169 degrees 31 minutes West. There we were welcomed by the military authorities. There were also Armored Personnel Carriers with machine guns pointed at us.

We were divided into groups of six, and I took notes and pictures about the Chemical Agents Destruction System.

That is what I was there for, and that is what they were telling me about. Of course I really didn't care about that at all. My main mission was the nuclear testing facilities, which were of crucial interest to the GRU. I used a special camera to take hundreds of pictures of the nuclear facilities. I supplemented the pictures with mental notes about locations, sizes, components, and so forth.

By the end of the day, I was trying to remember hundreds of details. I couldn't write them down because my notes might be examined. I mentally repeated the most important details to myself like a chant. At the same time, I had to interact with all the other correspondents in my group who were from America, New Zealand, and Australia, and I had to feign interest in the chemical destruction system.

At Fort DeRussy we were told that we would see a "live fire" demonstration. I noticed, however, that the artillery shells had broken caps, which meant that they were already used. That meant the system was not working properly.

I didn't mention this to the other reporters, but the system specialist noticed me looking at the bottom of the shells, and changed the topic of conversation. When we left the place, the specialist smiled at me and whispered, "Thanks for your silence, pal."

We spent about eight hours on the island, and I was impressed. Contrary to remote Soviet military bases, where the government really didn't seem to care about the soldiers, the American soldiers and civilians on Johnston Island seemed to live comfortably. There were good houses with every appliance. There were dining rooms for both the enlisted men and the officers. The Kon Tiki Officers' Club had a very good library and a very well stocked bar. They had very good exercise equipment, and a marina and golf course that was available for free to all residents of the island. Indeed the military seemed very solicitous about the well-being of the civilian population on the island. I have been located in some remote bases before—some much closer to Moscow than Johnston Island was to anywhere near the U.S. mainland—and I never knew soldiers could have it so good.

We went back to Honolulu that evening on the same C-141 that took us there. Thanks to the State Department officials, I had just enough time to run back to my hotel, grab my things, and check out. I barely caught my flight. Everyone was already on board when I got there, except for two FBI surveillance agents who were waiting for me.

The FBI agents followed me onto the plane and took their seats in the back, where FBI agents generally sit, to keep an eye on things. My seat was in the middle of the airplane, and I hoped that I would have some time to write down some notes about the nuclear facilities and clear my mind. It did happen, but a little later on.

This was a very unusual flight. In the first place, half the plane was a First Class section. There were also trees between the seats. It turned out the American Airlines CEO was on the flight celebrating the anniversary of American Airlines service to Hawaii. The captain announced drinks would be free, and the flight filled with very loud party music.

I tried to avoid these distractions and remember as much as I could, writing notes in my own little code. I also took time to write a legitimate story for TASS about the chemical destruction facility.

I finished writing my notes in the GRU field office. I sent them, along with the camera, to Moscow for processing. The camera was one of the GRU special self-destruct cameras that would have destroyed the film if some unauthorized person tried to open it. Apparently my mission was considered extremely successful. My boss and I received very special congratulations from the GRU Director himself.

I also received special congratulations from the TASS director general. My stories about Johnston Island, the Chemical Agents Destruction System, Honolulu, and American Airlines were considered extremely valuable to TASS. Never before had a Soviet reporter been able to report about such strange and exotic places that were virtually unknown to the Soviet people.

John later told me that U.S. counterintelligence was upset with him for booking me on the trip. But my stories in the Soviet press allayed their concerns, which shows how easy it is to fool even counterintelligence officers.

Many of the people whom I considered Trusted Persons were not Americans. The National Press Building had people from all over the world. I had friends from Korea, China, Japan, and many other countries. Usually these people had detailed information that was better than anything GRU officers inside those countries could get hold of.

Overall, I received information from about a dozen people. Only one of them was a "support agent." When *Spetznatz* troops carry out assassinations and terrorist acts in support of military operations, they needed a support infrastructure within the targeted country. "Support agents" provide safe houses and other general aid.

Peter was a security guard at the garage on the corner of 14th and H Streets, where TASS rented parking spaces for its correspondents. We, of course, knew that the FBI monitored the garage with "security" cameras.

One day Peter asked me to speak with him in a corner that was not monitored. He asked me if I was "really" with TASS. I said yes. He showed me documents with U.S. missile technology details, and asked me if I wanted to buy them. I said no, but that I would ask my friends if they knew anyone who would. I also asked him where he had gotten the documents. He said it was none of my business, and that he wanted at least $10,000 for it.

I took the documents back to the embassy, and the GRU resident sent a cable to Moscow. They authorized payment of $5,000. I met with Peter again and gave him the money. He then handed me another document and asked for more money. All the documents were related to missile technology. After handing over at least a dozen, he said that he had recently moved into a new home in Alexandria, Virginia, and found the documents in a box in his basement. The person who lived there before him was apparently an officer working in the Pentagon.

Since he was already willing to work with me, and unwittingly the GRU, I wanted to use him in another way, once he was out of classified documents. I convinced him to quit his job and take another job at a local gas station. Agents could then buy gas at the station and drop things off to him to pass on to me. He was the only support agent I managed, and I had to treat him in a specific, aloof way.

When I meet with espionage enthusiasts, they want to hear about all my covert exploits, secret meetings, and so on. The truth is that the more covert you have to be the less talented you are. The best spy will be everyone's best friend, not a shadowy figure in the corner. At least that's the way it is in an open country like the United States.

Chapter 15

A COUP IN MOSCOW,
A NEW LIFE IN AMERICA

ON THE MORNING OF AUGUST 19, 1991, Natalie roused me
with the words, "Wake up, there are tanks on the streets in
Moscow!" I had worked the night shift the night before and
had been to a party. I was tired, it was my day off, and I told
her she was joking and rolled over. Natalie shouted, "I'm not
joking! Look at the TV!" I sat upright and heard a voice say,
"Tanks in the street.... Military coup attempt.... Emergency
situation in the Soviet capital."

The first thing I saw was a Moscow street filled with tanks
and armored personnel carriers.

"It's impossible," is the first thing that I thought as CNN
started showing the self-appointed State Committee for
Emergency Situations (SCES). I saw the shaking hands of
the Soviet Vice President, Gennady Yanaev. I reminded
myself that I shouldn't be surprised. I had warned
Gorbachev through my reports to Moscow of this possibility,
even to the point of warning that if there were an attempt, it

would be on August 18 or 19. When it didn't occur on the 18th, I assumed that Gorbachev had derailed the plotters. But, no, everything was happening exactly as I had predicted.

And I had not been alone in my prediction. In July, U.S. Secretary of State James Baker warned Gorbachev, through official channels, that there might be a coup in the second half of August.

While I did not live in fear of an assassination attempt, I could not sleep without a loaded gun under my pillow.

My suspicious mind went into overdrive. Why, with all these warnings, had Gorbachev chosen this time to go on vacation to a small town on the Crimean peninsula—where he was now held hostage? I began to wonder whether Gorbachev might not be part of the coup. There were only two possible options. The first was that Gorbachev was an accomplice. If the coup succeeded, Gorbachev would become part of a new government formulated more to his liking as a "sign of good will." If it failed, he could still resume his job by posing as a victim. The other possibility, of course, was that he really was a victim. But why had he done nothing to ensure his own safety after receiving official warnings from the U.S. government and from the GRU? Personally, I did not believe that the SCES would last very long. The shaking hands of the vice president told me that they were cowards.

By the next day it was obvious the coup would fail. The SCES leaders were not appearing on the news. Soldiers were being attacked on the streets. And international leaders were throwing their support behind Boris Yeltsin and the Russian

Parliament, against whom the coup had been directed. By the third night, President Gorbachev was safely returned to Moscow.

The attempted coup actually helped solidify Yeltsin's power, as Gorbachev's slowly disintegrated over the next few weeks. Gorbachev made several governmental appointments, but they were soon replaced by Yeltsin appointees.

As the Soviet Union and then the Russian Federation fell into trouble, so did the GRU. The GRU never considered itself "the Assault Squadron of the Communist Party" as the KGB did. Protection of the Motherland, and not communist ideology, was our driving force. We did attend Communist Party meetings, but they were necessary evils and we accepted them as such. The GRU was there to protect the country and its people from our adversaries. Nothing more, nothing less.

> **Almost all of the GRU officers stationed in China with me have been diagnosed with cancer.**

Probably more important, we knew what was really going on inside the country. We knew that the USSR could not exist without "order" or a totalitarian regime, and when Gorbachev began his so-called reforms, he set in motion the dissolution of the Soviet government and its replacement by the only other organized power in the Soviet Union, the Russian mafia.

In March 1992 I made my own decision about how to deal with the death of my homeland. I defected. But many of my former friends and associates continued their intelligence activities for their new employer—the "new democratic" Russian Federation.

Others left the GRU for "commercial" endeavors. Between 1991 and 1995, 40 percent of all GRU operatives joined Russian companies that paid much better than the Russian Federation, but which are fronts for organized crime.

Indeed, Russia today is a criminal-capitalist state, in which those at the top do very well. In the early 1990s, the Israeli Mossad released a report claiming that the current Russian prime minister, up until March 23, 1998, Victor Chernomerdin, was the richest person in the world, through his shares of the Russian company, Gasprom.

On February 7, 1996, President Yeltsin ordered that industrial espionage become the top priority for Russian intelligence agencies. And the GRU is now putting all its efforts into recruiting agents from companies like Northrup, Gruman, GE, Honeywell, IBM, Microsoft, Bristol-Meyers Squibb, and countless others.

The goal, quite simply, is to hurt the American and international economies as much as possible, while filling the pockets of the Russian mafia and politicians. So in some respects, things have not changed that much. Russia is still trying to subvert the West, but now through economic rather than military and ideological means, and the ultimate goal is not the defense—or advance—of socialism and the Motherland; it is simply criminal profiteering.

To my mind, I am not a traitor. I was a loyal citizen of the Soviet Union, a country that was destroyed by traitors who dismembered the country for their own profit. The country I was sworn to defend no longer exists. The criminal regime that rules now is one I will not serve.

After I defected on March 25, 1992, I spent a year in a house in a gated community in Maryland, where I was debriefed by just about every major U.S. intelligence agency.

All of my debriefers were professional, and though I couldn't read their faces, I could tell they didn't trust me. Was I really a defector, or was I a plant?

This tore me apart. Here I was giving them everything they wanted, giving up my life as I knew it, and doing something that was punishable by death, and they didn't trust me. Nothing—not successful polygraphs, not anything—could erase their suspicion. I will have to live with this for the rest of my life.

I had to hide this feeling, just as I hid my fears of retaliation by the GRU. As a professional, I knew—and know— exactly how to carry out an assassination. I only hope that, if it comes down to that, my former associates will remember that they are soldiers and not murderers, and will kill me and leave my friends and family alone. Until recently, while I did not live in fear of an assassination attempt, I could not sleep without a loaded gun under my pillow.

After my debriefing, my "landlords" got me a job at Washington-based International Marketing, Incorporated, which was doing business in the former Soviet Republics. Part of my job was to recommend security procedures. Some of my customers followed my recommendations, and they are still in business. Some of them didn't, and they are going out of business. I also did briefings for the U.S. government and consulting to government and private institutions on Russian affairs and the dangers of Russian organized crime.

Eventually I came into contact with the Jamestown Foundation, which is a small, nonprofit think tank devoted to keeping the American people and their officials informed about what is going on inside the Soviet Union. And they put out newsletters. Journalism had been a major joy in my life while I was in the GRU, and I was delighted to be in it again. I wrote several articles for them, and looked forward to a long relationship with the Foundation.

But only God can make decisions for people.

I had a sore throat that wouldn't go away. I was diagnosed as having lymphoma, or cancer of the lymph nodes. This, I thought, was my punishment for everything I had done wrong in my life—for defecting from Russia, for betraying my friends, for being a spy in the first place, for not drinking extra milk while I was at Suvorov Military School, for not spending more time with my wife.... By the time I was finished, there was no reason why I shouldn't have cancer and drop dead on the spot.

Apparently I was not the only person who was stationed in Beijing to came down with cancer. In fact, I held out much longer than most of them. Almost all of the GRU officers stationed in China with me have been diagnosed with cancer. People assigned to the embassy had told me that they were picking up high levels of radiation from the apartment buildings around the embassy compound. Whether it was a form of high-tech monitoring or a conscious effort to harm our health, it seems to have been successful. So much so that in 1992 the GRU was asked to investigate the high rate of cancer among embassy officials. The findings, however, have never been made public; in part, no doubt, because of the rapprochement between Russia and China.

Since my chemotherapy and radiation treatments, I have written periodic articles and given lectures, and a few companies have hired me to assess their security. But by and large, American companies appear to consider security an unnecessary expense. They can't seem to believe that competitors and foreign intelligence agencies actually want to steal their secrets. But they do, and those who don't take precautions will pay the price.

I would like to close with three predictions or warnings— the sort of predictions or warnings I might have offered my former masters in the Kremlin, if I was still gathering and analyzing intelligence for them. I offer these predictions or warnings instead to the American people. My first prediction is that the Russian government will collapse in the near future. What happened in Russia on March 23, 1998 when Yeltsin fired his whole government, was only a cosmetic change. A future revolution *is* ahead. Its economy cannot support the pillaging, criminal overclass, which benefits only a tiny percentage of the people.

Corruption won't of itself destroy the Russian state, but crooked politicians and mobsters realize how hazardous the economy is and are sending their money abroad. The Russian mafia is a leech, sucking Russia's economy dry until it collapses.

My second warning is that the Russian mafia will become a major problem around the world. They will infiltrate any profitable market and are ruthless criminals. They have set up major operations in New York, California, and Florida.

Russian émigrés provide them with a vulnerable community to exploit and gain a foothold. Then they expand. Only a strong and diligent government can control their spread. The FBI will have its hands full.

The last warning concerns China. It has long been the world's sleeping giant. But no longer. Today, foreign companies are falling over themselves to invest in the country and the Chinese are implementing economic reforms. Unlike the Russian government, which was weak when it began its economic reforms, the Chinese government is strong and knows how to exploit its new success. Companies are so eager to gain entry to the Chinese market that they are willingly giving up important technological secrets in the process.

In recent standoffs, China has successfully faced down the United States—from Taiwan, to human rights, to arms sales, to extremely hostile nations. China has shrugged off American objections to its policies, and America has done nothing, because American companies want Chinese business.

In sheer numbers, China probably has the largest espionage web in the world. They also have the largest military forces. And their growing cooperation with Russia will only increase their threats and their arrogance toward America. The American public had better realize that China is going to be a major problem that is passed on to its children.

And finally, I should like to say that I am still searching for my real place in American society. I do so want to help this country that has graciously offered me a new life. In America there is hope. And I want to do what I can to preserve America's promise for the future.

DEBRIEFING ONE:
ISRAEL

ISRAEL HAS ALWAYS BEEN a special target for the Soviet intelligence services.

Operationally, GRU spying against Israel is managed by the Fourth GRU Directorate, in charge of Mideast and African countries.

Before Israel and the USSR normalized relations, most of the GRU mission was fulfilled outside of Israel, primarily in the Arab countries. Egypt was one of the Soviet Union's strongest allies in the area, and, conveniently, had the closest ties with Israel. Between the embassy, trade missions, cultural exchanges, and such, the Soviet Union had a huge presence in Egypt, which functioned as a launching point for numerous intelligence operations. Intelligence operations targeting Israel were, of course, also based in Syria, Lebanon, Iraq, Turkey, and many other states. And, surprisingly, the GRU had great success in recruiting Jewish citizens in Arab states to provide information on Israel.

During the Arab-Israeli wars, when Egypt and the Soviet Union were good friends, the GRU would regularly exchange intelligence with Egypt and other Arab countries. Among other things, the GRU provided military advisors that helped the Arabs improve their intelligence and military capability, and trained them to recruit agents as well.

There was also a special GRU branch specifically tasked with finding Russian Jewish emigrants who would spy for the Soviet government. Indeed, for some Russian Jews wanting to emigrate to Israel, spying for the Soviet Union was a condition of their release. In addition, some GRU officers emigrated to Israel under the cover of being Jewish.

After diplomatic relations were established between Israel and the Soviet Union, there was a scramble in the GRU to find officers who could staff the residency in Israel. The main qualification was knowing the Ivrit language, an Arab dialect.

The GRU actually had many Jews inside its ranks. But they had to hide or disavow their religion in order to be accepted into the intelligence services. If they were loyal to the Soviet Union, the GRU was happy to have them. But a secret directive issued by the Communist Party Central Committee stated that no Jews were to be allowed into the KGB or the Ministry of Defense's General Staff (the parent organization of the GRU). Soon after Boris Yeltsin took control of the Russian Federation and the Commonwealth of Independent States' Joint Military Command in early 1992, he decided to continue to exclude Jews from the GRU and other Russian Special Services.

The goal of the GRU residency is to infiltrate the Israeli military-political establishment, from the highest ranks of the government to the smallest field units. They want to know every detail about planning, strength, and operational capability.

More important, they want to collect economic intelligence—to steal Israel's scientific and industrial secrets. Israel has a very large research and development effort. Almost anything the GRU wants from the United States can be obtained through Israel.

Israel also has access to NATO and U.S. military technology and plans. As a close ally of the United States, the Israelis know a great deal about U.S. military systems and decisions. And many Israelis have close ties to American citizens, which can be exploited by the GRU.

The GRU recognizes Israel's military and political strength. Many GRU officers speak privately about the mistake the Soviets made when they decided to align themselves with the Arab countries instead of Israel. Israel, in their eyes, is not only strong, but also keeps its obligations, while many Arab countries do whatever is convenient or beneficial to them, regardless of agreements with their allies.

Like the KGB, the GRU has been thwarted time and time again by the Israeli intelligence services, the Shinbet and the Mossad. For a long time, the GRU did not even know the official name of the Shinbet. It is an incredibly effective organization that focuses on security issues. It gets little public notice but big secret results. Both organizations are incredibly effective, and man for man probably the best espionage and counterintelligence organizations in the world.

They have infiltrated the closed ranks of many terrorist organizations, which is truly impressive. The probable reason for their excellence is that they act as if their lives and those of their families were on the line every day. And, of course, to a large extent, they are correct.

A bigger problem for Israel is the Russian mafia. By utilizing the same emigration tactics as the Russian intelligence agencies, their numbers are growing inside Israel's borders. This is a major threat that Israel will have to deal with more actively. If the Israeli government doesn't make significant strides in halting the growth of organized crime, it could one day become a bigger threat than some of Israel's Arab neighbors.

DEBRIEFING TWO:
POWS IN VIETNAM

NO ISSUE HAS BEEN MORE SENSITIVE between the United States and the former USSR than the POW/MIA issue. Rumors that Americans are wallowing in KGB prison camps in Russia and Kazahkstan have never gone away. Prisoners from the Korean and Vietnam Wars were supposedly handled by Soviet military intelligence units and tortured for information or simply as punishment.

I was never sent to Vietnam, but I can relate what I know about this issue. When I was a teenager at the Suvorov Military School high in the mountains of the Northern Caucasus, we heard rumors that criminals assigned to death sentences and American POWs from the Korean War were working in the secret lead mines nearby. A few years later in the mid-1960s, when I was a student at the Tashkent Military Academy (the Soviet equivalent of West Point), there were rumors of American POWs working in the uranium mines in

Central Asia. There were also other rumors, but these were the ones that were repeated and stood out.

During the Vietnam War, rumors increased about hundreds of American POWs being brought into the Soviet Union via other countries to "Socialism Camps" where they would be used as human guinea pigs. Supposedly these people were subjected to nuclear, medical, climate, and other tests to see the effectiveness of new weapons of mass destruction. These poor souls were possibly subjected to chemical, seismic, biological, and other weapons to see how Americans physically differed from the Soviet prisoners that were subjected to the tests. There were also other rumors that American pilots were used to train Soviet pilots. For example, they would put an American pilot into a captured American plane and make him fly combat training missions against Soviet pilots. The airplanes were supposedly outfitted with special devices that prevented the airplanes from going too far, so the pilots couldn't escape.

Definitive confirmation of these stories is hard to come by. For many years the Soviet Union denied that they captured crew members from airplanes shot down during the Cold War. These denials were later shown to be false. In 1992 President Yeltsin stated that there were no Americans held against their will in Russia. But when Russia can't even keep track of nuclear weapons, there is little reason to believe they can keep track of Americans in KGB prison camps.

As a matter of fact Boris Yeltsin was shown contradicting himself on NBC's *Dateline* on June 16, 1992, saying that American POWs were possibly taken from Vietnam to the

Soviet Union. Later, Yeltsin's aides unofficially said Yeltsin was drunk and tried to discredit his comments.

There were several hearings held by the U.S. House National Security Subcommittee in 1996. During those hearings, Philip Corso, a former aide to President Eisenhower, testified that approximately nine hundred to one thousand-two hundred American POWs were sent by rail to the Soviet Union during the Korean War. In addition, another five hundred POWs who were ill were supposedly not returned during POW exchanges. According to Corso, many of the POWs were experimented upon and later executed. Possibly even worse, several KGB agents assumed the identities of some of the American POWs and were returned to American units for sabotage and other intelligence purposes.

Jan Sejna, a Czechoslovakian general who defected in 1968, also testified during those hearings. Sejna claimed that he saw American POWs in Prague, and saw orders saying that they were to be taken to Moscow for drug and radiation experiments. The KGB was interested, Sejna testified, in finding ways to worsen the drug problem in the United States.

This is not as far-fetched as many Americans would like to believe. I have heard KGB officers supporting these claims. Moreover, the KGB claims to have trained the Columbia drug cartels about money laundering, drug production, drug smuggling, and drug distribution, and also provided equipment and intelligence information.

Through my KGB and GRU contacts, I heard many stories of how Stalin and other leaders initiated many long-term efforts to undermine American society. Their main effort was to increase violence inside the United States, and their effort included paying selected Hollywood producers to produce violent and offensive films. The Soviet Union also provided financial support to the most aggressive and violent minority leaders. The Soviet Union always supported "agents of influence" who could either sway people to the Soviet point of view or cause general turmoil in the United States.

The Vietnam War was considered a major GRU success. In fact, the GRU believes it won the war. The GRU funded every major antiwar group. Any antiwar activists who claim otherwise are sadly naïve. Of course the support often came through third parties or was otherwise disguised, but the Soviet Union pumped more than twice as much money into the antiwar campaign as it did to North Vietnamese military and economic support. The success for the GRU was that not only did their influence help win the Vietnam War, but they tore apart the entire social fabric of the United States and made military service a mark of shame.

Now I want to tell the public what I have also told to Senate investigators about the MIA/POW issues, including possible scenarios based on what I had been told by other well-informed sources.

The Soviet military presence in North Vietnam included dozens of GRU officers, perhaps a few dozen KGB officers, *Spetznatz* troops, Soviet military units maintaining anti-aircraft batteries, and representatives from the Ministry of Defense and the General Staff.

GRU officers served as Military Advisors to the Vietnamese intelligence services, providing battlefield intelligence assistance and helping to identify American POWs who might cooperate with Vietnam or the Soviet Union. If they found an American who agreed to cooperate they could train him how to spy in Vietnam, and might send him to Russia for advanced training. Then the GRU would arrange his escape from a POW camp or have him released during a POW exchange.

However, trainees who could not complete their training or were thought to be faking their cooperation, would be given to the KGB. If the KGB was unsuccessful in reforming them, the prisoners would be sent to secured prison camps in the Soviet Union and most likely their death.

At these camps, people could be killed for no reason. Some prisoners were given the choice of working in Soviet uranium and plutonium mines for five years, which is as good as a death sentence. It is also rumored that the KGB transferred some failed agents to mental asylums. The POWs were kept in solitary confinement until they died.

Soviet involvement was highly sensitive. The GRU assigned officers with Asian features to Vietnam. They were often given Vietnamese uniforms and integrated directly into the Vietnamese units. They trained many Vietnamese about how to interrogate people and obtain cooperation.

As far as the torture of American prisoners goes, the GRU would not have been involved with this. The Vietnamese had everything they needed to get tactical information out of people. All it required was attaching electrodes to the genitals of American prisoners and giving a few cranks on the generator of a field radio. The Vietnamese also had truth serum provided to them by the GRU. The GRU might identify prisoners who had highly valuable information, but it was left to the Vietnamese to get the information out of them.

POWs who failed to cooperate or who were selected to become agents were left to the Vietnamese to deal with.

So to sum up, the GRU's primary purpose in Vietnam was to recruit possible agents. If they had a possible agent, they would attempt to train him and possibly send him to Russia for advanced training. Then his "escape" or POW transfer was secured. If he was unsuccessfully trained, he was likely turned over to the KGB for further handling. This meant he was sent to a KGB prison camp in the Soviet Union and probable death. While this is based on second-hand sources and I cannot confirm it, it is in total agreement with standard GRU and KGB doctrine.

Perhaps the most telltale sign of GRU involvement is the fact that any officers who were stationed in Vietnam have never been allowed outside of the Soviet Union, which is extremely unusual and, for a spy's mind, suspicious.

INDEX

adultery, 74

Afghanistan War, 28, 123

alcohol, 81, 123, 126

America the enemy, 37, 43, 48, 50, 79

Americans: loyalty, 79; naive, 86; agents, getting, 79, 140–41

American Civil War, 31

ANADYIR, *see* Cuban Missile Crisis

Andrews Air Force Base, 145

assassination tactics, 11, 32, 160

Aum Shinrykyo, 32, 81

Baker, James, 156

Baltic State Technical University, 20

Berodzkov, Alex, 138

black market, Russian, 14, 91, 123

Black Sea coast, 36

Blinov, Arthur, 101

brainwashing, 31

Brezhnev, Leonid, 54

Budapest, 58

Bush, George, 139

Charda, 107

Chechnya, 28

China: relations with foreigners, 110; USSR and, 13, 74, 100, 108, 121; U.S. and 162; growth of, 162; counterintelligence, 114, 103–04, 121–22; standard of life in, 101–03

Chimkent, uprising in, 54
Chop, Ukrain, 57
CIA, 11, *see also* counter-
  intelligence
"clean duties," 129–30, 132, 135
Clinton, President Bill, 18
computers, 13
Cold War, 11, 22–23, 28
counterintelligence: U.S., 79,
  105, 137, 151; Soviet, 74, 82
Cuban Missile Crisis, 27, 44–47
Czechoslovakia, 107

Dayan, Moshe, 54–55
Deep Reconnaissance
  Company, 59
disinformation, 47, 53, 55, 168
Draba, 104–05
drop sights, 25–27, 76, 137
drugs, 169

Egypt, 54, 164
espionage devices, 13, 76–77,
  80, 144, 151
economic war, 158
ethics, 31
explosives, 29, 76

FBI, 11, 17, 127–29, *see also*
  counterintelligence
Fedorovich, Sergei, 66–69
Feinbert, Ludwig, 17

First Subdirectorate, 95–100
Fort DeRussy, Hawaii, 147–49
Fotigarov, German, 130–132
France, 81
FSB, 20

Gorbachev, Michael, 14, 28,
  123, 155–157
Gore, Vice President Al, 18
Glavnoye Razvedyvatelnoe
  Upravlenie (GRU): 11, 12,
  14, 19, 22, 25, 27–28, 32;
  activities of, 23, 24, 29; effect
  of coup, 158; efficiency, 85;
  entrance into, 72, 74–77; propaganda, 47; structure, 79,
  95–96; terrorists and, 80–81
Gulf War, 32

hackers, 13
Hickam Air Force Base, 148–49
Higgins, Lieutenant Colonel,
  139
Hungary, 57, 62
Hussein, Saddam, 20, 32

internet, 13
Iran, 2, 20–21
Iranian Sanam Industries
  Group, 20
Iraq, 19
Israel, 81, 163–65

Italy, 81
Ivanovich, Colonel Yuri, 88
Ivashutin, General, 97

Jamestown Foundation, 160

Kalachev, Evgeni, 105–06
Kennedy, 46
KGB: 11, 23, 28, 51, 130, 169; propaganda, 47; GRU, 138, 74, 106; standard of living, 84–85; terrorists, 80
Khaddafi, Moammar, 21
Khrushchev, 46, 47
Korean War, 167
Krisheev, Gennadi, 103
Kronstadt, 17
Lamar, 91–92
Lebed, Alexander, 25
Lenin Military Political Academy, 63
Libya, 21
Loutchanski, Grigori, 18
Lunev, Stanislav: defection, 157; family life, 41–42, 61; ideology 61–62, 65, 157; interests, 41, 43, 48, 86; introduction to GRU, 67–69; law school, 61, 63, 66; recruiting, 75, 104–109, 111–120, 134–36; reporter, 96–100, 122; Spetznatz, 60–61;

upbringing and training, 35–39, 41, 48, 49, 50, 55, 60

mafia, Russian: 11, 12, 161, 166; capitalistic, 14; in America, 15–22
Manhattan Project, 28
Manolo, 107
Marxism, 50, 65
Maslennikov, Ilya, 99
Mastrukov, Oleg, 104
Mescheryakov, Colonel, 46
MDG, 82
MGB, 36
Military Diplomatic Academy (MDA), 70
Ministry of State Security (MGB), 36
Molchanov, Vladimir, 121

Nazis, 37
North Korea, 21
nuclear weapons, 2, 12, 24–27, 46

oil, 20
Operation Desert Shield, 144
Operation Desert Storm, 31, 144

Pakistan, terrorism, 81
Paper Agents, 104

perestroika, 14
Pilishchaba, 58–59
poisen, 11, 29
Pol Pot, 109
propaganda, 78, 86
prostitution, 16–17

Rabinovich, Vadim, 18
Rank, Michael, 110
Rashidov, Sharaf, 54
Reagan, Ronald, 14
recruiting process, 12, 13, 23,
    91–93, 106
Reserve Officers Training
    Course, 90
Romyntsev, Gennadi, 121–22
Russia, see USSR
Russian Ministry of Defense
    Industry, 13–14
Russian Space Agency, 20

security: U.S., 12–13, 129, 131,
    152–153; Soviet, 70–72, 74,
    95, 97
Sergeev, Colonel Igor, 96, 97
Sergeevich, Igor, 74
Shevtsov, Leonid, 99
Singapore, recruiting in, 88, 90
Six Day War, Israel, 54
smuggling, 26
Sochi, 36
Solovie, Vasili, 104 v, 105

Soviet Union, see USSR
Spetznatz: 22, 23–24, 27–28;
    during war, 29–30 duties of,
    59; train terrorists, 32, 151,
    170
Stalin, Joseph, 36
Suvorov Military School,
    38–39, 41, 42
Suvorov, Alexander, 38
SVR, 12, 14, 20
Syria, 21

terrorism, 19, 32–33, 80, 81,
    139
"Trusted Person," 104, 108
Turkey, terrorism, 81
Trubnikov, Vyacheslav, 20
Takhta-Bazaar, 50–52
Tashkent, 49, 52–53

United States: middle class,
    125; recruites, 152; reaction
    to Islamic terrorism, 142;
    targets, 29–30
USSR: allies, 32; army, 60, 62;
    China relations, 13, 74, 100,
    108; collapse of, 12,
    155–161; commerce, 19;
    Czechoslovakia relations,
    107; Hungary relations, 57,
    62; living standard, 62, 83;
    Mid East relations, 19, 21,

54, 163–64; stupidity of, 73,
88–89, 130; technicians,
21–22; treatment of prisoners, 168–69; U.S. relations,
22, 37, 43, 125, 169

Vavilov, Colonel, 97
Verlin, Evgeni, 103
Victorov, Captain, 87
Vietnam, 60, 78, 167–72
Vladikavkaz Infantry Academy,
42

weapons, 28–31, 144–50
wives, Soviet, 72
World Trade Center bombing,
32, 81

Yakovlev, 139
Yakushev, Lieutenant Colonel,
43
Yanaev, Gennady, 155
Yeltsin, Boris, 12, 28, 36, 156,
158, 164, 168
Yellow Book, 132–33

Zhuchin, Yudgin, 70, 72, 73, 82